ROOSEVELT and DANIELS
A Friendship in Politics

Roosevelt and Daniels

A FRIENDSHIP IN POLITICS

Edited with an Introduction
by
CARROLL KILPATRICK

— CHAPEL HILL —
The University of North Carolina Press

For
FRANCES

✒ INTRODUCTION ✒

Franklin D. Roosevelt, age thirty, and Josephus Daniels, age
fifty, first met in Baltimore at the Democratic National Convention of 1912 and helped bring about the nomination for
president of Woodrow Wilson. It was an auspicious occasion
for them both. Daniels was one of the most active and influ-
ential of the Wilson men present and played a leading role
in the Convention that almost nominated Champ Clark of
Missouri, candidate of the conservatives, but finally, on the
forty-sixth ballot, nominated Wilson. Young Roosevelt, then
a New York State Senator, was already a man full of confidence and high spirits. But his role at Baltimore was not an
important one. He was, however, for Wilson.

Roosevelt called on Daniels with a group of New York
editors seeking press tickets. It was their first meeting and
it marked the beginning of a friendship that was unique in
American politics and extended over a period of more than
thirty years. The older man, who served in the administra-
tions of Cleveland, Wilson, and Roosevelt, outlived the
younger one by three years, but the younger man was four
times elected President of the United States. Politicians have
little time for friendships that are not useful to them, and
few friendships in politics extend over three decades. The
Roosevelt-Daniels friendship, however, genuine though it became, was useful to both men and, as time went on, it took
on the aspects of a father-son relationship. Roosevelt and

Daniels became friends despite some serious handicaps, and they remained friends despite some serious disagreements. The letters tell the story.

The early years of the friendship were the most difficult, when the differences in age, social and economic background, temperament, and ideas were most pronounced. But the friendship carried them safely through the two terms of Woodrow Wilson, when Daniels was Secretary of the Navy and Roosevelt Assistant Secretary. It saw them through the twelve years of Republican rule, when each was playing a significant part in the up-hill efforts to revive the Democratic Party by an alliance of the radical West and South and the reform East. Finally, the friendship brought the men together again when the younger one was President and the older his Ambassador to Mexico.

Few men were ever more unlike than Daniels and Roosevelt. Daniels was the small-town editor from the South, an economic radical who distrusted show and sophistication and was generally hated by the Carolina power and railroad magnates. Roosevelt was the aristocrat from the North, who attended Groton and Harvard and never knew poverty. In his early years, Roosevelt was bright and attractive and very much the privileged man of society. The instinct for reform developed in him comparatively early; the instinct for liberalism and economic experiment became manifest later. Nothing is so clear in the early days as the fact that Roosevelt belonged tightly to his class. During the first years of the Wilson administration, Roosevelt was active socially and he had many Republican friends in Washington. His letters during this period contain more than one contemptuous reference to the idealism and humanitarianism of Daniels and William Jennings Bryan.

Daniels, on the other hand, had crusaded with Bryan long before F.D.R. could vote. In those days, Bryan was a terror more fearsome to the Eastern capitalists than F.D.R. ever became. In a letter to this writer in 1951, Mrs. Eleanor Roosevelt said that "in the long run" the relationship between Daniels and her husband "was a close and a warm one." She wrote that as "my husband grew older he was able to appreciate how really fine Mr. Daniels was and Mr. Daniels became mellower as he grew older and was a more liberal person than he had been in his youth." Daniels may have grown mellower and more tolerant; but he was a liberal—"radical" is a better word—long before F.D.R. was. Daniels had been fighting the trusts and the economic royalists even before T.R. got into the fight. Daniels' Raleigh *News and Observer* battled the trusts on home ground and they in turn put up money for two or three papers in Raleigh to try to run Daniels out of business. Daniels was a member of the left wing of the Democratic Party, which was the Bryan wing and the decisive force in the nomination and election of Wilson in 1912.

Another difference between the New Yorker and the North Carolinian was that one was a lawyer, the other an editor. They are two different breeds of men. A lawyer likes to get things done, to figure out the details of a problem and to institute action. An editor is fundamentally a philosopher, a man who often ponders a problem for a long time before acting. He is seldom a good administrator. The editor quickly recognized the lawyer's ability to get things done. In 1932, after Roosevelt had been nominated for the presidency, Daniels wrote that the two words which best described F.D.R. were "eagerness" and "determination." To those, he said, should be added "personal charm" and "ambition." The best words to describe Daniels are "puritan" and "democrat," to which might be added "homely virtues" and "sentimentalist."

On another occasion, Daniels said that if he were asked by what rule Franklin Roosevelt sought to regulate his life he would answer that "his philosophy is along the line laid down by the Sage of Craigenputtock, old Thomas Carlyle, who wrote: 'On the whole, a man must not complain of his "element," of his "time" or the like; it is thriftless work doing so. His time is bad: well then, he is there to make it better.' " [1]

The letters between Roosevelt and Daniels, particularly those of the Navy period, show the young Roosevelt as an impetuous and often brilliant man of action, impatient with the slower-moving Daniels and with the tradition-bound senior Navy officers. During his early months as Assistant Secretary of the Navy, Roosevelt took pleasure in mimicking Daniels before his friends of the Metropolitan Club. Roosevelt often wrote memos to the older man which showed an astounding lack of tact and respect. But as time went on, he learned to appreciate the strong points in Daniels' character. The influence of the Southerner was humanizing and Daniels introduced Roosevelt to a type of American he had hardly known before—a type that was to become all-important in the fulfillment of his soaring ambition. Unlike Roosevelt, Daniels was full of moral fervor. He was a Methodist and

1. Josephus Daniels, *The Wilson Era, Years of Peace* (Chapel Hill, The University of North Carolina Press, 1944), p. 133.

a prohibitionist, two factors which gave a different coloration to his radicalism from that which Roosevelt later espoused as the New Deal.

After their first meeting at the Baltimore Convention, the two men saw each other occasionally during the 1912 presidential race. Daniels was in New York City that summer and fall as Director of Publicity for the Wilson campaign, and Roosevelt, who was a candidate for re-election to the State Senate, stopped in a few times to see him. Like Wilson, F.D.R. was victorious when the votes were counted in November.

As Wilson began planning his Cabinet, he first thought of offering Daniels the postmaster generalship in recognition of his political ability but changed his mind and made him Secretary of the Navy. It was easy to criticize the appointment, for Daniels had no special knowledge of the Navy and his politics made him suspect as far as the Admirals and conservative leaders of the country were concerned. But Daniels' first decision was a good one: it was to ask F.D.R., who loved the sea and had studied naval history, to be his Assistant Secretary. There were several reasons why Daniels turned to F.D.R. Roosevelt was an important name and F.D.R. was, after his two victories for the State Senate from a normally Republican district, clearly a rising star in New York politics. Another reason was that Roosevelt was a Northerner. Also, his distant cousin, Theodore Roosevelt, once had been Assistant Secretary of the Navy. Daniels was convinced that he and Roosevelt would complement each other well.

Years later, Daniels told how he offered the post to F.D.R. "As I entered the Willard Hotel on the morning of Wilson's inauguration," Daniels wrote in one of his autobiographical volumes, "I ran into Franklin Roosevelt. I had not seen him since the election. He was bubbling over with enthusiasm at the incoming of a Democratic administration and keen as a boy to take in the inauguration ceremonies. He greeted me cordially and said, 'Your appointment as Secretary of the Navy made me happy. I congratulate you and the President and the country.' I responded by asking him, 'How would you like to come to Washington as Assistant Secretary of the Navy?' His face beamed his pleasure. He replied, 'How would I like it? I'd like it bully well. It would please me better than anything in the world. I'd be glad to be connected with the new administration. All my life I have loved ships and have been a student of the Navy, and the assistant secretaryship is the one place, above all others, I would love to hold.' " [2]

William Gibbs McAdoo, who was to be Secretary of the Treasury, already had offered Roosevelt a position in the Treasury Department. But the Navy was clearly his first choice. Daniels explained that he had not consulted Wilson about the appointment but that he would do so at the first opportunity. Wilson knew little of Roosevelt, but, two days after the inauguration, when Daniels placed the name before him, gave his assent. The President sent the nomination to the Senate on March 12, 1913.

Senator James A. O'Gorman, a Democrat from New York whom Roosevelt had supported, accepted the appointment without much show of enthusiasm. Senator Elihu Root, a New York Republican whom Daniels was not bound to consult but whom he did consult as a courtesy to the Senator,

2. Daniels, *The Wilson Era, Years of Peace,* p. 124.

told Daniels, "You know the Roosevelts, don't you? Whenever a Roosevelt rides he wishes to ride in front." [3] It was an observation that Daniels must have remembered frequently in the months that followed.

Root recalled that Secretary of the Navy John D. Long had not found it easy to work with Assistant Secretary Theodore Roosevelt. But of F.D.R., Root said, "I know the young man very slightly but all I know about him is creditable and his appointment will be satisfactory so far as I am concerned, though, of course, being a Republican, I have no right to make any suggestion. I appreciate your courtesy in consulting me." Daniels said he replied that he was not afraid of having a strong assistant, and remarked, "A chief who fears that an assistant will outrank him is not fit to be chief."

Daniels' thoughtfulness in consulting Root was typical of his attitude toward Congress. He was nearly always on good terms with the great majority of the men on Capitol Hill. Daniels' experience in politics and with politicians—he was one of the leaders at the Baltimore Convention who never lost faith that Wilson would be nominated—made him an invaluable administration leader in relations with Congress. Roosevelt was able to learn from Daniels much about Congress and the ways and prejudices of politicians. Also, Roosevelt was able to learn about the small-town middle-American, and the problems, the sympathies, and the points of view of the American farmer and worker, whom Daniels knew as well as he knew his congressmen.

Daniels had lived close to the soil. He knew the farmers and workers and politicians of a small community. He was born in Washington, N. C., on May 18, 1862, when North

3. Daniels, *The Wilson Era, Years of Peace*, p. 127.

Carolina was fighting as a Confederate State. Eighteen years later he began his editorial career on the Wilson, N. C., *Advance*, published at the seat of the Wilson Collegiate Institute, where Daniels attended school. He was vehemently Democratic and democratic even in those days. Early in life, he said, he vowed never to belong to any organization which was not open to everybody. "That left open to me," he wrote, "only two organizations to my liking—the Methodist Church and the Democratic Party." [4] After the inauguration of President James A. Garfield, Daniels' widowed mother lost her job as postmistress at Wilson because of her son's anti-Republican editorials.

In 1885 Daniels moved to the capital of his State to become editor of the Raleigh *State Chronicle*, a weekly which he published for five years. He was always ambitious to have a daily, however, and on March 6, 1890, announced that the *State Chronicle* "would take a forward movement and become a daily paper" committed to "an increased warfare on trusts and monopolies, the freeing of farmers and laborers from unjust taxation, hostility to special privileges in all forms ... and the universal education of the people of North Carolina." Unfortunately, the daily did not succeed financially, and Daniels was forced to sell it. Thereupon he established the weekly *North Carolinian*, which he published even during an interlude in Washington during the second Cleveland administration, when he was Chief Clerk of the Interior Department, a position comparable to that of Assistant Secretary today. In 1894 Daniels heard that *The News and Observer*, which had been losing money, was to be sold at

4. Josephus Daniels, *Tar Heel Editor* (Chapel Hill, The University of North Carolina Press, 1939), p. 243.

auction. He was determined to buy it, but he knew that the tobacco and railroad interests would block his purchase. Through the intervention of a friend, a lawyer was retained to bid on the paper for him, and Daniels purchased the daily paper in the capital of North Carolina for $6,810.

Daniels had long had his eyes on *The News and Observer,* a paper which he made a powerful voice in North Carolina politics and which still is in his family. Despite his own forays into politics, Daniels always remained an editor at heart and was the active editor of *The News and Observer* until his death a few weeks before his eighty-sixth birthday. He was always a prolific writer both of news and of editorials.

After his death in 1948, the vast collection of his papers was presented to the Library of Congress by his sons, Josephus Daniels, Jr., Dr. Worth B. Daniels, Jonathan W. Daniels, and Frank A. Daniels. The papers fill 960 containers, number approximately half a million pieces, and take up 410 linear feet of shelf space. Most of the letters in this book were found in the Daniels collection at the Library of Congress. The others were found at the Franklin D. Roosevelt Library at Hyde Park. The majority of the letters are in both collections.

Not all of the Roosevelt-Daniels correspondence is included in this volume. But most of it is. All of the letters that seemed to be significant or interesting are included. A few have been cut to eliminate unimportant detail. Nearly all of the corrspondence of the Navy period, other than some routine office communications, is included. Nearly all of the correspondence after the Navy period has been included with two exceptions: a few letters from F.D.R. which are still not open because they refer adversely to a living person and some of Daniels' letters from Mexico that are very long and detailed and of little general interest. All of the Daniels letters were made available for use. Some of the correspondence has been lost despite the care which both men took to preserve everything they wrote.

The chief interest of the volume will be for the Roosevelt students and all those who are fascinated by the Roosevelt personality and character. The letters cover most of his mature life. But the Daniels' letters are revealing, too. Josephus Daniels was a man in his own right, a leader in his state and nation for more than half a century, a type of editor and public official too seldom found in America today.

❧ CONTENTS ❧

ROOSEVELT and DANIELS
A Friendship in Politics

THE NAVY YEARS

MY DEAR MR. ROOSEVELT:

I have made inquiries about the necessary qualifications for a secretary in your office and I find that so far the men who have been there have been stenographers.

However, there is another clerk in that office who is a stenographer and you may find you can get along with him for any dictation you want, so I want you to suit yourself about your private secretary.

JOSEPHUS DANIELS

WASHINGTON, March 11, 1913

MY DEAR MR. ROOSEVELT:

Your appointment will be sent to the Senate tomorrow. I had a very pleasant talk with Senator Root about it, and you will be gratified to know that he says it will be a very acceptable appointment to him and to the State. I will wire you as soon as the appointment is confirmed and hope you can come on at once. I look forward with great pleasure to the association with you which the acceptance of this position makes possible.

Sincerely yours,
JOSEPHUS DANIELS

[Elihu Root, who had been Secretary of War in the cabinet of President William McKinley and Secretary of State in the cabinet of President Theodore Roosevelt, was a Republican Senator from New York from 1909 to 1915. Daniels also consulted Senator James A. O'Gorman, a Democrat. Neither Root nor O'Gorman objected to the appointment, but neither approved of it very heartily.]

ALBANY, March 12th, 1913

MY DEAR MR. SECRETARY:

I am very glad to hear that the appointment is to go to the Senate today and I am gratified to know that it is acceptable to Senator Root. As soon as I hear from you I will leave for Washington and will be there in any event on Friday morning early.

I do not need to tell you again how very much I am looking forward to the association with you.

Very sincerely yours,
FRANKLIN D. ROOSEVELT

WASHINGTON, March 17, 1913

TELEGRAM TO ROOSEVELT

You have been confirmed.

JOSEPHUS DANIELS

Roosevelt, having resigned from the State Senate, was accompanied to Washington by Louis McHenry Howe, the former Albany newspaper man who had joined F.D.R. as a political guide and sponsor and had managed his 1912 campaign. Howe was to remain with Roosevelt until he was safely in the White House two decades later. Like Daniels, Howe had a great influence on F.D.R., teaching him many facts of political life and making him see that his appeal had to be to many segments in the population.

When Roosevelt took the oath of office as Assistant Secretary of the Navy, he was only thirty-one years old. But he was not at all frightened by the job. If anything, he was entirely too confident of his ability, ready to take on any responsibility and to handle any assignment.

WASHINGTON, April 30, 1913

MY DEAR MR. ROOSEVELT:

I am enclosing a schedule of my southern trip so that you will know just where to get me by telegraph in case anything of importance happens about which I should know. If any important matter comes up that needs my attention before May 13th, you can communicate with me fully by telegraph.

At Raleigh, N. C., you can get me at my own house and the other places at which I shall stop are noted on the margin.

Faithfully yours,

JOSEPHUS DANIELS

[Daniels left Washington on April 30 to visit Raleigh, Jacksonville, New Orleans, Pensacola, Key West, Charleston, Port Royal, and Savannah. He returned to Washington on May 13.]

WASHINGTON, July 29, 1913

MY DEAR MR. DANIELS:

Things have been going on from day to day so uneventfully since you left that I have not written you before.

The Southern Pacific gentleman, as you have probably read, is safe in Guaymas, and I at once telegraphed this information to the president of the road. Mr. Hinds was not under restraint at any time but, having crossed over from the insurrecto to the federal lines, the federals refused to let him pass back again.

This morning your telegram came about the fuel oil for Bremerton. I have gone to the bottom of the matter during the past few days, and think the Bureau of Yards and Docks may eventually prove to have been wrong in its technical working out of oil values. The Union Oil Company bid was eighty-nine cents, while that of the Standard Oil Company was ninety cents a barrel; but the Bureau unanimously recommended the ninety cent bid on the ground of much superior quality, less water, etc. In this case I could not delay the matter to re-advertise, as the supply is very low and something had to be done at once. I have, however, invited the Union Oil Company to prove their contention.

The Mexican situation is really the only matter to disturb our quiet existence. In the past week there has been a very noticeable change of feeling in Administration and Congressional circles. It is being regarded as a very threatening and imminent danger. Ambassador Wilson has talked steadily since he landed.

Next week the fleet holds its joint maneuvers with the Army off Block Island, and I am planning to go up for a few days about the time you return and to inspect the Newport station at the same time. If, however, I have to leave before you get here, I will leave a memorandum of anything of importance, and I should not be gone for more than a week.

I hope you and Mrs. Daniels have not had it very hot. On the whole, we have had pretty cool weather since you left. You are much missed, and Mr. Banks is wandering around like a lost soul in Israel.

With kind regards to you both,

Very sincerely yours,

FRANKLIN D. ROOSEVELT

["The Southern Pacific gentleman" may have been Charles De Lano Hines, who was Senior Vice President and general manager of the Southern Pacific Railroad in Mexico during 1912-1913. The "Mexican situation" was one of violence and confusion following the overthrow of Porfirio Díaz in 1911 by Francisco Madero, who was in turn overthrown by Victoriano Huerta and shot. The United States refused to recognize Huerta. Henry Lane Wilson had been Ambassador to Mexico since 1909. President Wilson retained the Ambassador but soon lost confidence in his ability to report objectively on the turbulent situation in Mexico. His resignation, therefore, was accepted in August, 1913. On August 27 President Wilson addressed a Joint Session of Congress on "Mexican Affairs," urging a policy of friendly neutrality. Howard Banks was Daniels' private secretary.]

WASHINGTON, August 7, 1913

MY DEAR MR. ROOSEVELT:

I have given orders today that the *Dolphin* shall be in Poughkeepsie on August 19th for the celebration of the Independent Order of Odd Fellows.

I hope you will find it convenient to go up in her from New York, as I prefer to have you on board rather than have her go alone. In my opinion it would be a rather bad precedent to have her attending celebrations like this unless she is taking some one in authority along, as other cities would then begin to call for her presence at such celebrations as this.

Very sincerely,
JOSEPHUS DANIELS

[The *Dolphin* was the Secretary of the Navy's yacht.]

A short time after Daniels and Roosevelt had begun work together, in the old State, War and Navy Building across West Executive Avenue from the White House, they were asked to pose for pictures. They stood together on the portico looking toward the White House. The photographer got an excellent picture of the two men, one always prized by Daniels. When it was brought in for approval, the following exchange, according to Daniels, occurred:

" 'Franklin, why are you grinning from ear to ear, looking as pleased as if the world were yours, while I, satisfied and happy, have no such smile on my face?'

"He said he did not know of any particular reason, only that he was trying to look his best.

" 'I will tell you,' I answered. 'We are both looking down on the White House and you are saying to yourself, being a New Yorker, 'Some day I will be living in that house'— while I, being from the South, know I must be satisfied with no such ambition.'

"We both laughed as we returned to our desks. Later, when he was in the White House, he recalled the event, and we both preserve copies of that autographed photograph, taken when we were young and consecrated to a great task." [1]

WASHINGTON, December 23, 1913

MY DEAR MR. ROOSEVELT:

I am sending you a photograph taken on board the *Wyoming* during our visit to the fleet at target practice, which I hope you will keep as a souvenir of the trip.

With hearty good wishes for the New Year to you and Mrs. Roosevelt, in which Mrs. Daniels joins, I am,

Sincerely yours,

JOSEPHUS DANIELS

[Daniels, Roosevelt, and a large number of officials went to Hampton Roads in October, 1913, to inspect a fleet of nine battleships before they left for a Mediterranean cruise.]

WASHINGTON, December 24, 1913

MY DEAR SECRETARY:

Many thanks for the photograph you sent me as a Christmas remembrance. It will serve as a very artistic remembrance of an exceedingly pleasant trip and I cannot tell you how much I was pleased at receiving it. I, too, am having a photo made for you, but unfortunately it will not be ready until New Year's. It is a copy of a very delightful old water color of the U.S.S. *North Carolina* taken, I should judge, about 1850 and I thought it would be of peculiar interest to you.

Wishing you very many returns of what I trust will be an exceedingly pleasant Christmastide, believe me,

Very sincerely yours,

FRANKLIN D. ROOSEVELT

1. Daniels, *The Wilson Era, Years of Peace*, p. 129.

The following is from Daniels' diary:

"My most prized Christmas present was a painting of the U.S.S. *North Carolina* which Franklin Roosevelt had ordered for me. It is the work of a famous artist. Franklin had the record showing that it was the first American line-of-battle ship to cross the Atlantic. She made that voyage in 1825. She returned to New York from her last voyage in 1839, and was finally sold in 1867 for $30,000. She was built at the Philadelphia Navy Yard and launched in September, 1820."

WASHINGTON, January 28, 1914

MY DEAR MR. ROOSEVELT:

You cannot know how much I value the beautiful picture of the *North Carolina* which you sent me. Nothing could have given me more pleasure. I will keep it and transmit it to one of my sons and also transmit to all of them the affection and regard I bear to you. When I came to Washington one of the anticipated pleasures was the close association with you. As yoke-fellows this association has been both helpful and delightful. I wish you to know my regard and appreciation of you as a man and as a fellow worker.

Faithfully your friend,

JOSEPHUS DANIELS

On August 2, 1914, F.D.R. wrote a long letter to his wife complaining about the slowness of Daniels and William Jennings Bryan, the Secretary of State, in recognizing the implications of the European conflict. "To my astonishment on reaching the Dept.," Roosevelt wrote, "nobody seemed the least bit excited about the European crisis—Mr. Daniels feeling chiefly very sad that his faith in human nature and civilization and similar idealistic nonsense was receiving such a rude shock." [2]

Roosevelt had been visiting his family at Eastport, Maine, when the Navy Department telegraphed him late in July that war in Europe seemed likely and requested him to return to Washington. Years later, at a press conference in the White House at which he announced his lend-lease program, Roosevelt recalled the earlier experience. At the lend-lease press conference, on December 17, 1940, Roosevelt was concerned about reports that the Western powers could not continue fighting, because of a lack of money. Those reports reminded him, Roosevelt said, of his 1914 trip back to Washington on the Bar Harbor Express. "I went into the smoking room," he reminisced. "The smoking room of the express was filled with gentlemen from banking and brokerage offices in New York, most of whom were old friends of mine; and they began giving me their opinion about impending war in Europe. These eminent bankers and brokers assured me, and made it good with bets, that there wasn't enough money in all the world to carry on a European war for more than three months—bets at even money; that the bankers would stop the war within six months—odds of 2 to 1; that it was humanly impossible—physically impossible—for a European war to last for six months—odds of 4 to 1; and so forth and so on. Well, actually, I suppose I must have won those—they were small, five-dollar bets—I must have made a hundred dollars. I wish I had bet a lot more.

"There was the best economic opinion in the world that the continuance of war was absolutely dependent on money in the bank. Well, you know what happened."

As Assistant Secretary of the Navy, Roosevelt was impetuous, as his cousin Theodore was, and believed that America

2. F. D. R., *His Personal Letters, 1905-1928*, ed. Elliott Roosevelt (New York, Duell, Sloan and Pearce, 1948), p. 238.

should take an active part in the fighting. It is noteworthy that in the early days of World War I Roosevelt, paying little attention to public opinion, wanted to push the unwilling nation into war. In the early days of World War II, Roosevelt, the responsible political leader, moved one step at a time, always fearful lest public opinion not keep up with him.

"These dear good people like W.J.B. and J.D. have as much conception of what a general European war means as Elliott has of higher mathematics," F.D.R. wrote his wife five days after Austria-Hungary declared war on Serbia and one day after Germany declared war on Russia. France entered the war the next day, August 3, and Great Britain at midnight on August 4.

During the early days of the war, Roosevelt had many Republican friends in Washington. He was often in touch with Theodore Roosevelt, a savage critic of Wilson, Bryan, and Daniels. F.D.R. had to discover the hard way later that preparedness is as much a matter of the unity of the country as a matter of guns and ships.

Well before war broke out in Europe, Congress, acting under the spur of Wilson and Daniels, authorized the construction of five new battleships. "We shall take leave to be strong upon the seas," Wilson had said in his 1914 State of the Union message. The two years that followed that message, Daniels said, were the busiest the Navy had ever known in time of peace. Daniels was for peace in 1914 but he was also for a big navy.

On August 5, in another letter to his wife, F.D.R. wrote: "Alive and very well and keen about everything. *I* am *running* the real work, although Josephus is here! He is bewildered by it all, very sweet but very sad!" (Note Roosevelt's frequent use of exclamation points, a habit that stayed with him all his life.)

Again his supreme confidence in himself and his impatience
with the slower-moving Daniels are shown. Nowhere in the
Daniels' papers, it should be recorded, is any rancor shown
toward F.D.R. Yet Daniels must have known that the younger
man mimicked him and was not entirely loyal. Roosevelt was
not, however, insubordinate in the sense that his cousin
Theodore might have been in a similar situation. Many years
later, Daniels contented himself with this comment about
Roosevelt: "He was young then and made some mistakes.
Upon reflection, although I was older, I made mistakes too." [3]

EASTPORT, MAINE, August 18, 1914

TELEGRAM TO DANIELS

Future admiral arrived last night. Everything all right.
Both doing splendidly.

FRANKLIN D. ROOSEVELT

[Franklin Delano Roosevelt, Jr., was born August 17,
1914.]

WASHINGTON, August 18, 1914

TELEGRAM TO ROOSEVELT

Congratulations to the young senator and his mother.

JOSEPHUS DANIELS

WASHINGTON, August 20, 1914

MY DEAR MR. ROOSEVELT:

Everybody in the office wondered why the moon shone so
brightly and the night of August 17th was so extremely
pleasant until your telegram of the 18th explained the cir-
cumstances. We all send our heartiest congratulations. My

3. Daniels, *The Wilson Era, Years of Peace*, p. 129.

wife sends love to Mrs. R. and the young—Senator or Admiral?

Faithfully yours,
JOSEPHUS DANIELS

EASTPORT, MAINE, August 24, 1914

MY DEAR MR. DANIELS:

Everything is going well up here and the baby is splendid. We have had very cool weather and a good deal of fog and rain. I do hope you will be able to get off even for a few days on the *Dolphin*, and you must be sure to let me know in case you are able to cruise as far along the coast as this out of the way spot.

I am planning to leave here about the 3rd or 4th of September and am telegraphing today to ask you to send a destroyer up here the 2nd. I will then go down in her as far as Boston, inspecting East Lemoine and Portsmouth on the way. This will get me back to Washington on the 7th. I hear very little political news, but certainly hope the report that Hearst is to run against me is true. It raises my fighting and sporting blood to think of a campaign against that person.

With our warmest regards to you all,

Faithfully yours,
FRANKLIN D. ROOSEVELT

In 1914, against Daniels' advice, F.D.R. was persuaded by Secretary of the Treasury McAdoo and other administration leaders to become a candidate for the United States Senate. Daniels did not believe Roosevelt could win the nomination or that the Democrats could win the election. Roosevelt, however, had been an enthusiastic anti-Tammany Democrat and the Wilson men were eager to deal a death blow to the organization. Roosevelt became a candidate but failed to win the nomination. James W. Gerard, then Ambassador to Germany, defeated him by a two to one vote. Gerard was defeated in the election by the Republican candidate, James W. Wadsworth, Jr.

WASHINGTON, August 26, 1914

DEAR MR. ROOSEVELT: [at Eastport, Maine]

We have in contemplation the opening of the New Orleans Navy Yard in the near future and have tried to get from your files any conclusions that you may have reached from your inspection of that Yard and in the study of the Department's files. We find, however, only a collection of documents bearing on the general subject of the Yard treated from the position of the Board of Inspection for Shore Stations and from that of the local interests. If you had reached any conclusions in the matter, these we have found no trace of. My purpose is to inquire whether you have any such written conclusions and where they may be found. If not, and you have formulated any such conclusions in your own mind, will you please jot them down, even in a rough outline, and send them on to help us in the matter.

I find on examination of the chart of the New Orleans Yard that by utilizing Buildings 10 and 11 and part of the administration building five hundred marines can be comfortably quartered there without interfering with the industrial activities of the Yard—at least, up to the capacity of the floating dry dock. To provide for more than five hundred marines, it would be necessary to destroy in part or entirely some of the industrial equipment.

It seems to me that for the present it would be best to spend about twenty-five or thirty thousand dollars in remodeling Buildings 10 and 11 for five hundred marines whenever they are returned from Mexico. This would not mean that they should be returned to New Orleans, but first given leave up north to visit their homes. By the time that had been finished the buildings would be ready at New Orleans for their occupancy.

May I ask for an early reply?

Sincerely yours,

JOSEPHUS DANIELS

WASHINGTON, August 28, 1914

MY DEAR MR. ROOSEVELT:

Your letter of the 24th inst. brings gratifying news. We are all delighted to know all is well within your household. Mrs. Daniels wishes to be remembered most cordially to Mrs. Roosevelt. We both had hoped to see you all and render our obeisance to the "Commodore," before the month expired, but it has become apparent we must abandon the cruise. I am still obligated to the Lake Champlain engagements, but will go North direct and by rail to the point of my first engagement.

The destroyer has been ordered to meet you on the second. I'm glad you're going to visit Portsmouth and Boston en route home.

With warmest regards from everyone at Single Oak to everyone at Eastport.

Yours sincerely,

JOSEPHUS DANIELS

EASTPORT, MAINE, August 29, 1914

MY DEAR MR. DANIELS:

The only memorandum in writing which I have prepared about New Orleans is the proposed notice to the Press and a copy of which was on my desk when I left the Department. I enclose, however, a short report which you can use if you think it advisable to show that the question of opening the yard has been thoroughly gone over for some time.

Of course, the opening of the yard for industrial purposes would hardly be justified if it were used only for the repair of half a dozen gunboats and surveying ships permanently stationed in the Gulf and Caribbean. I think it is absolutely essential that there should be in addition a well defined amount of work done for the Army and Treasury and Commerce craft on the Mississippi and in the Gulf, and I would, therefore, suggest that you personally get Mr. Garrison, Mr. McAdoo and Mr. Redfield to cut the red tape in their own departments and insure the repair of their vessels by us. We have had favorable replies, as I remember it, from the War Department and the Treasury Department, but unless the Secretaries push it themselves we cannot be sure that the work will actually be given us to do.

I agree entirely that buildings ten and eleven and part of the administration building should be put in such shape that the yard can house 500 marines. This will have the further advantage of concentrating the industrial work into quarters commensurate with its needs and importance.

Very sincerely yours,

FRANKLIN D. ROOSEVELT

[Lindley M. Garrison was Secretary of War from 1913 to 1916. William G. McAdoo was Secretary of the Treasury from 1913 to 1918. William C. Redfield was Secretary of Commerce from 1913 to 1919.]

WASHINGTON, September 10, 1914

DEAR MR. DANIELS:

The Wage Board at the Washington Yard on May 12th last believed that the wages of the core makers should be increased by eight cents, giving a maximum of $3.68 and a minimum of $2.64. This was in line with their previous recommendation. On May 19th, after talking with you, I sent word that the case would not be reopened during that fiscal year. Now, however, we are in another fiscal year and I believe it would be just to allow this very slight increase to go into effect even at the present time, as it has been recommended ever since last January.

Very sincerely yours,

FRANKLIN D. ROOSEVELT

In a speech many years later, F.D.R. described some of his labor duties in the Navy Department. After he had been in office only a week, he said, a delegation from the Brooklyn Navy Yard came to see him, and the spokesman for the delegation said, "You know, as Assistant Secretary, you have statutory charge of all labor matters." Roosevelt replied, "That is fine; I did not know it." He said he established a "perfectly practical example of collective bargaining," which prevented any major labor disputes in the Navy yards during the Wilson administration.

Mrs. Roosevelt's comment on this period is significant: "Franklin's job in the Navy Department was, I believe, one of the milestones in his life. It would have been easy for him to have become just a nice young society man.... This was

Franklin's first close contact with labor; and there is no doubt, as I have said, that it was one of the turning points in his development." [4]

WASHINGTON, March 16, 1915

DEAR MR. DANIELS:

I attended the meeting of the General Board this morning and we discussed in every phase the proposal to hold the war game this Spring off the coast. Some of the members of the General Board seemed afraid that such a war game would seem too belligerent in view of existing international conditions. I assured them, however, that it was quite sufficient to leave this phase of the matter in the hands of the President and yourself. . . .

In my judgment, as I told you, the maneuvers should make a definite impression on the minds of the "men in the streets." This can be done without impairing their value to the Navy itself, and, also, such a war game would be, I think, very valuable in correlating the work between the fleet and the Department, as would be necessary in time of war. This is, of course, absolutely in line with the proposed reorganization of the Division of Operations.

I think the General Board began to see the light, although in the beginning they spent most of their time talking politics. They are now drawing up a new plan which I think will be satisfactory. This plan will probably involve merely the addition of a second phase to the original plan.

Whatever you decide on I think it important that the Department (and the War Department if they join us) should

4. Eleanor Roosevelt, *This I Remember* (New York, Harper & Brothers, 1949), p. 23.

appoint an official reporter, or censor, who would give out an official statement of what had actually taken place. This would prevent any erroneous statements in the press or misconceptions of the purpose of the plan.

I am off in a few hours and everything is quiet. I will go over the Division of Operations matter with great care and have something ready when I get back.

With my warmest regards,

Faithfully yours,
FRANKLIN D. ROOSEVELT

P.S. I have seen a copy of the General Board's so-called "administrative section" of the general war plans. This is one of the matters which it is, I think, very important to take up soon.

[Shortly after writing this letter, Roosevelt left with his wife to attend the Panama-Pacific International Exposition in San Francisco.]

TYRONE, N. M., April 5, 1915

TELEGRAM TO DANIELS

Arrive Saturday morning. Very successful trip. Have several new suggestions regarding organization of operations and hope I can submit them before definite action taken.

ROOSEVELT

[The Roosevelts stopped off for a visit in New Mexico en route home after their trip to San Francisco.]

WASHINGTON, April 5, 1915

TELEGRAM TO ROOSEVELT

Glad to see you Saturday and talk matter over. No action will be taken until afterward.

JOSEPHUS DANIELS

The correspondence for this period is very small. Apparently the relations between the two men were at a low point, as the above telegrams suggest. In May they went to New York for a Navy League banquet. Daniels spoke in high praise of the "forward-looking Sixty-third Congress." Roosevelt, on the other hand, implied that Congress wasn't moving ahead on preparedness measures with sufficient speed. "Most of our citizens," the Assistant Secretary said in a tone that showed little faith in the people, "don't know what national defense means. ... Let us learn to trust to the judgment of the real experts, the naval officers."

On June 8 William Jennings Bryan resigned as Secretary of State because he believed Wilson's stern second note to Germany regarding the sinking of the *Lusitania* would lead to war. Daniels did not believe the note would lead to war.

WASHINGTON, July 1, 1915

MY DEAR FRIEND:

The doctor has just telephoned me that your temperature is normal, that you came out from the operation in fine shape, and that there is no reason why I should stay. You know my plan was to get three days at the seashore with my family, but had decided to postpone the trip after you went to the hospital. But now that your mother is here and you are getting on so well I will run down to North Carolina and stay till Tuesday morning. My plans are made then to remain in Washington during the month of July. You can, therefore, make your arrangements to go to Maine as soon as the doctor will let you travel, feeling perfectly free, and it will be a pleasure to me to remain on deck. You will need the salt air and bracing climate after your stay in the hospital. For the present, you need to rest and sleep, with your mother near you. Your friends will look for your early getting out and ready for play.

With my love and happiness that you are coming on so finely.

Sincerely your friend,

JOSEPHUS DANIELS

[On July 1, Roosevelt was operated on for acute appendicitis.]

WASHINGTON, July 23, 1915

DEAR ROOSEVELT:

I hope you had a comfortable trip up to your home and continue to improve. The General Board is holding daily sessions now considering the program and policy. I have asked Admiral Badger to remain on the Board after his retirement until we complete the plans and the report is ready. The spirit in the Board and in the Department is all that could be desired, everybody working harmoniously. The President is going to recommend a constructive program and I think Congress will cooperate. Enclosed is a copy of a letter from the President which Badger read to the Board today. It is fine and will be most helpful.

The Advisory Board or Committee seems to be universally approved and I believe we will get good results.

The hard nut to crack is navy yards. We need improvement and economy and I hope you will put your mind on the things we ought to do about navy yards. I am enclosing a letter from Naval Constructor Robert. He worked to succeed Capt. Bryan. I frankly told him we were thinking of letting that place go into innocuous desuetude, but would be glad to have his views and suggestions. In response to that, he sent the enclosed. I do not mean to impose any work on you until you are well, but thought as you were improving this would interest you.

Everything is running along well. Will let you hear occasionally. Remember me with warm regards to your wife (tell her to be strictly neutral) and to your mother if she is with you.

Sincerely,

JOSEPHUS DANIELS

[Rear Admiral Charles J. Badger was head of the Navy's General Board. Captain (later Rear Admiral) Benjamin C. Bryan was director of Navy Yards from 1912 to 1915. Captain (later Rear Admiral) William P. Robert was in the construction corps during World War I.]

EASTPORT, MAINE, August 3, 1915

MY DEAR MR. DANIELS:

Many thanks for your letter. I am glad everything is going well and I am delighted to see the President's letter. As you know, I have felt for quite a long time that a good many people —more than have appeared on the surface—in the Republican and Progressive parties are going to take advantage of the national preparedness issue this Fall and also next year, basing this on what is becoming an increasingly strong public opinion on this subject. And I have felt that the administration must recognize this, not only in general terms, but by coming forward with a definite program. . . .

There are two fundamentals which I think we can safely assume. First, the European war has shown that the old theory of abolishing navy yards is, under modern conditions, wrong and that we should maintain every existing Government plant, running it as economically as possible in time of peace, but in such a way that it can in the event of war be readily expanded to the utmost capacity. In the event of war we should find use for every plant now under the Navy Department. Secondly, very decided improvements can be made in the organization of the navy yards. This applies to the actual management of the yards through a central body and also to the actual work performed by the individual yards. At the present time each yard practically runs itself on its own lines, as it sees fit, and turns out any kind of work it wishes.

I am writing to McGowan to ask him to prepare for me a complete list of every *kind* of work performed in each yard. As soon as I get back I want to have a series of conferences with McGowan, Taylor, Griffin, Captain McKean and Admiral Benson, in order that we can submit a fairly definite plan. This conference can be entirely formal or can be in the nature of a formal board, as you think best. Personally I believe that we can devise a plan which will save an appreciable amount of money or give us an increased output, which is the same thing.

I am getting on very well, but still have to go slow in the way of exercise. But unless war breaks out in the meantime with Germany, Mexico, Santo Domingo or Haiti I am planning to leave here on the 13th and you can count on me being at the Department on the morning of the 16th. I hope you have been able to get some rest, but I fear this horrid affair in Haiti has kept you very busy. Give my very warm regards to your wife, as we both hope you will all be able to come up the coast of Maine in August and that you will not fail to come as far as Eastport. I fear you have had great heat in Washington and you must not fail to telegraph me if I can be of any help, because I am really quite able to come to Washington from now on at any time.

Always faithfully yours,
FRANKLIN D. ROOSEVELT

[Because of unrest in Haiti—seven Haitian presidents were assassinated between 1911 and 1915—and the fear that Germany might attempt to establish bases for U-boats in this area near the Canal Zone, the Navy was ordered, in August, 1915, to restore and maintain order in Haiti and Santo Domingo. Brigadier General Smedley Butler commanded the Marines who landed in the islands. Rear Admiral Samuel McGowan was Paymaster General. Rear Admiral David W. Taylor was Chief of the Bureau of Construction and Repair from 1914 to 1922. Rear Admiral Robert S. Griffin was chief of the Bureau of Steam Engineering. Captain (later Vice Admiral) J. S. McKean was assigned to the Department in 1915. In 1919, he was for a short time Assistant Chief of Operations. Admiral William S. Benson was Chief of Naval Operations from 1915 to 1919.]

EASTPORT, MAINE, August 7, 1915
MY DEAR MR. DANIELS:

I am enclosing a letter which Andrew Peters sent me in regard to another candidate for the advisory board. He sounds as if he had enough qualifications for it at least.

It is certainly a curious coincidence that as soon as I go away we seem to land marines somewhere. Everything seems to be going well, however, in Haiti and I trust there will be no more fighting.

Everything is going well up here. Mr. McCarthy has arrived and I am trying to catch up with my work.

With my warmest regards,

Always faithfully yours,

FRANKLIN D. ROOSEVELT

[Andrew Peters was the Democratic Mayor of Boston during the famous strike of the city's policemen in 1919. Charles H. McCarthy was secretary to Roosevelt.]

On a memo sheet of the Office of the Assistant Secretary is an undated longhand exchange between the Assistant Secretary and the Secretary. It presumably is in connection with some formal function which neither wanted to attend:

SECNAV—

It would be unseemly for the ass. sec. to head the list.

ASS. SEC.

I think this is one case in which the asst. secy should take the lead. Go the limit!

JD

I always obey orders worse luck.

FDR

Another undated pencilled memorandum exchanged between the two follows:

SECNAV—

1. I beg to report

(a) That I have just signed a requisition (with 4 copies attached) calling for purchase of 8 carpet tacks.

ASTNAV

Why this wanton extravagance? I am sure that two would suffice.

J.D.

Washington, February 16, 1916

Dear Mr. Daniels:

I have looked over the most pressing of my mail for the first time in ten days. The most pressing part of that part relates to the proposed naval training cruise.

As you know, this is something I have worked up for months with great care and in all its phases—naval, political and civilian. As you know, I consider it of almost vital importance from all three standpoints—naval, civilian and political.

The training cruise, as proposed, does not require authority from Congress. If the cruise is to be held this summer definite announcement of it should be made at once. It should have been made three weeks ago.

I fear you have some kind of an idea that the cruise will be taken advantage of only by college boys, rich young men, well-to-do yachtmen, etc. I want to remind you of the fact that I have twice been elected to office in a fairly large and cosmopolitan kind of district and that I can rightly claim to be in touch with every element in the community. You may, therefore, I think, with perfect propriety accept my word for it that the proposed naval training cruise would be carried out on absolutely democratic lines.

In regard to Blue's reserve bill, you will doubtless remember his enthusiasm a year ago for his naval reserve bill and my statement to you at that time that his bill was all right as far as it went, but that I doubted if he got 500 men in the reserve during the first year. I understand that at the present time he has got about 300. I think, therefore, that you will recognize that my guess may be fairly good, and I state that his proposed reserve bill will undoubtedly get a certain number of sea-faring men in the coastwise trade into the ranks of the reserve; that possibly, aside from his suggested voluntary reserve, he may get ultimately 8,000 or 10,000 men, but that if we are to have a real reserve in this country we must start the ball rolling by building up INTEREST.

The only way we can build up interest at the present time is by establishing a training cruise.

Such a cruise can be established this summer, but only if it is announced now.

Excuse this long letter, but I have been trying to get something on this for three whole months and I do not want to feel that my illness is delaying it.

F.D.R.

[Rear Admiral Victor Blue was Chief of the Bureau of Navigation and very close to Daniels.]

This letter, written with some asperity, shows Roosevelt's impatience with anyone who stands in his way once he has made up his mind something ought to be done. Daniels often moved slowly, much to Roosevelt's annoyance. At the time the letter was written Roosevelt was suffering from a throat infection. Many years later, when Roosevelt was President and his good health was much talked about, Daniels remarked privately that during the Navy years Roosevelt seemed to catch every bug that came along.

WASHINGTON, Feb. 17, 1916

DEAR ROOSEVELT:

I am happy to know that you are steadily improving and hope you will soon be yourself.

The idea of using the ships for civilians was presented to the Council and all favored it and as soon as you get well we will work out the plan. I gave Blue your notes and he is working on it.

My wife is sending you a partridge and hopes you will enjoy it. Love to all the family.

Sincerely,

JOSEPHUS DANIELS

WASHINGTON, August 21, 1916

MY DEAR ROOSEVELT:

Referring to our conversation the other day about the *Dolphin*, it is unnecessary for me to tell you that I would love to do what you wished but I fear that it would not be the part of wisdom to do it. Mr. Padgett came in to see me this morning and said he would like to have the *Dolphin* for a few days. I told him certainly he was the Chairman of the Naval Committee, but I pointed out the possibility of criticism, asked him to think it over and he has just now informed me that he feels it would not be wise at this time, there are so many crazy people. As you know I have sent my boys to Raleigh for the same reason. I could not get away to go with them on the *Dolphin*, combining official duty with a pleasure trip, so rather than risk adverse criticism I gave it up entirely. Don't you think it would be a mistake at this time to send the *Dolphin* into Maine upon anything except an official trip?

Cordially yours,

JOSEPHUS DANIELS

[Lemuel Phillips Padgett, who also had wanted to use the *Dolphin*, was a member of Congress from Tennessee and Chairman of the House Naval Affairs Committee.]

Daniels was always much more careful than Roosevelt not to take small liberties that he might have taken because of his position. At the end of the war, F.D.R. offered to have one of Daniels' sons sent home ahead of some of the other men in his unit. Daniels immediately ordered Roosevelt not to give any special treatment to a Daniels. While Roosevelt followed a strict moral code in many things, he often used his official position to aid members of his family. His own attitude toward Daniels' refusal to allow him to use the *Dolphin* is revealed in a letter of August 18 to his wife, in which he said that Daniels had been accused in Congress of intending to use the *Dolphin* to campaign in Maine—hence was "scared blue and *Dolphin* won't be allowed within 1000 miles of Maine till after September 11." Then Daniels was planning to use the *Dolphin* for a week or two and "I might get her about the 20th. I am really upset at the thought of bringing you all down by rail." [5]

A month later, after the Maine elections had been held, Roosevelt was able to get the *Dolphin* to move his family from Campobello to Hyde Park. There was a polio epidemic that year and he thought the children would be safer not to travel by train.

5. *F. D. R., His Personal Letters, 1905-1928*, ed. Elliott Roosevelt (New York, Duell, Sloan and Pearce, 1948), p. 325.

WASHINGTON, October 14, 1916

MY DEAR ROOSEVELT:

I understand that some of the ship-building companies may come to see you to ask a further postponement of the date of opening of the bids, or ask the Department to commit itself in advance in regard to possible modifications of contract.

I do not wish any change whatever made. We will probably have trouble anyway.

Please decline any requests and say that bids must be had on the date already set upon.

Sincerely yours,

JOSEPHUS DANIELS

[On August 29 Congress had authorized the construction of 157 war vessels—ten battleships, six battle cruisers, ten scout cruisers, fifty destroyers and many lesser craft. Bids were advertised for the next day. "Before the end of 1916, we had entered upon the biggest shipbuilding program ever undertaken by any navy at one time," Daniels wrote later.[6]]

WASHINGTON, October 24, 1916

MY DEAR CHIEF:

Everything has been smooth sailing since you left and I am here for the first three days of this week, leaving on Wednesday for Long Island, Rhode Island and New York, returning next Monday again.

In regard to the names, I think the names for the new battleships have met with a good response. In the case of renaming the armored cruisers, there has been no difficulty with three of them. Seattle was logical, because it is not only the biggest city

6. Daniels, *Our Navy at War* (Washington, D. C., Pictorial Bureau, 1922), p. 13.

in Washington but because the Chamber of Commerce and various other bodies there sent long telegrams asking that it be done. In the case of West Virginia, Huntington was logical, because it is the second city of the State in population and we already have a *Wheeling* named for the biggest city and a *Charleston*. In the case of Colorado, Pueblo was, as you know already, the only possible choice.

But in the case of Maryland I am somewhat up a tree and am withholding the announcement of that name until I hear from you. Congressman Talbott wants the armored cruiser named Towson. I am ashamed to say that I never heard of Towson before! It turns out that it is the Congressman's county town—twenty-five hundred inhabitants—but really a suburb of Baltimore, the buildings being practically continuous between the two. I fear that we would get into a good deal of trouble if we took that name. About the only two places in Maryland that are possible, it seems to me, are Hagerstown and Frederick. We already have an *Annapolis* and *Cumberland*, and I have turned down the suggestion of certain people in the Department that she be called the Chevy Chase! I hate to go against Talbott's wishes, but suppose the best thing to do is to do nothing for a while and I have merely told him that I would take the matter up with you.

I spent last Friday and Saturday up-State New York and am really encouraged, especially by the swing of the farmers. In certain districts it will be wise to start the cry of "get on the bandwagon" by the beginning of next week.

Always faithfully yours,

Franklin D. Roosevelt

[Daniels was on a trip in the Middle West. J. Fred Talbott was a Democratic congressman from Maryland.]

WASHINGTON, February 10, 1917

MEMORANDUM FOR THE SECRETARY:

1. I find that we have six 6-inch guns (Mark IX, 44 calibers long) which are regularly held for the American Line Steamer *St. Louis*

2. I have talked to Admiral Earle and find that we have no authority to sell serviceable ordnance material and, while these guns are somewhat old, it would be in the nature of a subterfuge to condemn them and sell them as condemned material at present. Under the law, however, guns may be *loaned* provided a suitable bond be given.

3. Frankly I believe that an intolerable situation is beginning to arise. After my investigations in New York yesterday it is clear that American ships cannot get guns suitable for arming themselves except from the government, and I believe the position of the American Line is well taken—that they cannot square it with their conscience to let their passenger ships leave New York without some protection, either convoyed or armed.

4. The situation is now this: The Navy has enough guns to let the American Line and other larger ships have two large guns for each ship. (It is really a fact that the 3-inch guns are too small for use against submarines). I would suggest that we can properly loan these guns with their mounts and ammunition. The work of installation and mounting of the guns to be by the owners of the vessels. This I am confident they can do themselves.

5. May I ask that you send this memorandum to the President, as I believe it points a way out of the difficulty of asking the authority of Congress? The special point I would make is that the only available guns are in the possession of the United States Government. If we refuse to let this source become

available to private companies we close absolutely the only door open to them. We have taken the position that it is entirely proper for merchant ships to arm if they so desire. We can, therefore, by loaning these guns, give them the only opportunity to get them and they themselves would be entirely responsible for the installation and handling of the guns after they are on board. In case this should be approved it would take four or five days' work before the vessels could be made ready to sail and in the meantime, as you know, everything is held up.

FRANKLIN D. ROOSEVELT

[Rear Admiral Ralph Earle was Chief of the Bureau of Ordnance.]

The second point of this memorandum will sound familiar to those who remember Roosevelt's lend-lease proposal in late 1940. Whether he himself remembered his 1917 plan when he proposed lend-lease is not known, but his memory was always remarkable and the suggestion of 1917 may have stuck in the back of his head. The memorandum shows again F.D.R.'s ability to cut through red tape in an effort to get things done. "The late Josephus Daniels once told me," says John Gunther in his *Roosevelt in Retrospect*, "that of all Roosevelt's qualities he put agility of mind first, even ahead of charm and courage."

WASHINGTON, March 10, 1917

TELEGRAM TO ROOSEVELT IN NEW YORK CITY

Please see Mr. C. V. Van Anda Managing Editor of New York Times and obtain his views with reference to securing cooperation regarding the non-publication of articles which might be disadvantageous. Also please see Admiral Usher who will acquaint you with situation.

JOSEPHUS DANIELS

[Rear Admiral Nathaniel Reilly Usher was Commander of the New York Naval Yard from 1914 to 1918.]

WASHINGTON, April 4, 1917

MEMORANDUM FOR THE SECRETARY

1. I am entirely dissatisfied with the manner in which the Bureaus of Construction and Repair and Steam Engineering and the Division of Operations have handled the whole subject of constructing Chasers.... Attention is now invited most solemnly to the fact that the Navy Department will be held responsible for the policing and patrol of the entire coast of the United States from *now* on, and without waiting until next autumn ... I believe this is a matter of such importance that it should be taken up and decided within twenty-four hours. I believe that we should go ahead at once with the construction of all possible additional vessels which could be made use of. ... If we wait much longer the date of delivery will go through to 1919.

FRANKLIN D. ROOSEVELT

Two days after the memo above was written, Congress declared war on Germany. There was an early scare that U-boats would attack New York. According to Daniels, Roosevelt shared that fear and made a tentative contract to build 50-foot motor boats to patrol the harbor. Neither Daniels nor the construction officers of the Navy favored building the 50-foot craft. Later, 110-foot boats were built.

Shortly before receiving Roosevelt's urgent memo of April 4, Daniels recorded in his diary: "Franklin Roosevelt urged more motor boats to be used for patrol. Will order many but are they valuable? How much of that sort of junk should we buy? Admiral Taylor, ablest naval construction officer in the world, and Admiral Rodman thought it money unwisely expended. Roosevelt was intent upon having many for use in harbors. In my heart I agreed with Taylor and Rodman. But suppose U-boats should enter our harbors and we lacked patrol boats, what then? Contrary to my belief in their worth I told F.D.R. to go ahead and buy a number."

[Rear Admiral David W. Taylor was chief of the Bureau of Construction and Repair from 1914 to 1922. Rear Admiral Hugh Rodman was a member of the Navy's General Board in 1917.]

WASHINGTON, April 1917

DEAR MR. DANIELS:

Do please get through two vital things *today:*

1. Get that Interior Building or give it to War Dept. & let us take latter's space here.

2. Authorize calling out Naval Militia or Reserve—It is essential to get them if we are to go ahead.

FDR

[At the top of the above note to Daniels is the following notation in pencil: "Do you always follow his advice?" The penciled note is not in Daniels' hand.]

In a similar vein, an undated note on Roosevelt's office memo pad says:

"*The actual present* danger of this situation should be explained to the Secretary and he must understand that *immediate* legislation is necessary—if it is delayed we can and should be indicted for murder first degree, if one of these places goes up in smoke."

WASHINGTON, April 18, 1917

MEMORANDUM FOR THE SECRETARY:

Just for your own information, I want to call to your attention the fact that it is two weeks since the awards were made to private companies for building the 110-foot patrol boats, and that I am told today by Naval Constructor Furer and the Bureau of Supplies & Accounts that not one single contract has been signed. They say that the contracts in every case but one have been sent to the builders, but again I want to call attention to what I have many times repeated, that at least half of these bidders cannot be called responsible firms with adequate equipment for the work, and again I want to prophesy that we are going to fall down very sadly in the actual delivery of these boats at the times and in the numbers we expect.

In other words, while 340 have been ostensibly ordered, it is my personal judgment that we won't get anything like this number, and that we ought without question to build many additional boats, preferably of larger size and of steel, and build them now in carshops and other factories which will not interfere with the regular steel shipbuilding industry. This *can* be done and the boats will begin to be delivered in 7 months, but it *cannot* be done if it is handled along Bureau routine lines like the case of the 110-footers. Today is April 18th, nearly three months after the definite need became evident and, except in the case of one or two navy yards, practically not a timber that will go into their construction has been sawed.

FRANKLIN D. ROOSEVELT

On June 26, 1917, Roosevelt sent Daniels a long memo on his visits to the first, second, and third naval districts. He reported conditions good at the first, matters in the second "thoroughly unsatisfactory." He found conditions in the third very bad and said that since mid-April he had begged that reforms be made. "As I have many times recommended, the organization of the Naval District Defense should be radically changed," he wrote. "I have for nearly two months insisted that the work was going badly, and certain officers in the Division of Operations have admitted as much, but these officers frankly have failed utterly to remedy the conditions. It is all very well for them to admit that change and improvements are necessary, but I should like to see the change and improvement take place. Meanwhile the days, and the weeks and the months, are piling up and I should very much like to see some definite action taken."

WASHINGTON, July 12, 1917

MEMORANDUM FOR THE SECRETARY

Before these estimates go to Congress, or are submitted by you to the President, I want to urge most strongly that two items be added.

(1) If we are going to build any more *destroyers*, no matter what type, *the estimates should go in now, whether the number be 50, or 100, or 200.*

(2) Decision should be made and the estimates submitted on the question of building *additional wooden submarine chasers*. In the absence of the formation and adoption of a new naval policy along offensive lines, it is to be assumed that the present policy of chasing submarines all over the ocean will be adhered to. If this assumption is correct, units, i.e. *numbers, necessarily count,* and for this you have in this country organizations now running, navy yards and private plants, for turning out wooden

chasers. If the Department is going to build any additional wooden chasers, *contracts should be let before September 1st,* in order that the material may be obtained in time to prevent the disintegration of the existing private organizations, which must necessarily be dissolved about November unless additional work is given them.

FRANKLIN D. ROOSEVELT

WASHINGTON, September 7, 1917

MEMORANDUM FOR THE SECRETARY

On June 21st, 22nd, and 23rd, I made an inspection of the First, Second, and Third Naval Districts and immediately thereafter gave you a memorandum setting forth certain conditions in regard to materiel, personnel, and the military operations of the districts. I pointed out that the conditions as a whole were not satisfactory....

Three days ago I returned from a second inspection trip.... As a result of this trip taken over two months after my first trip, I am sorry to say that the conditions are to all intents and purposes no better....

FRANKLIN D. ROOSEVELT

WASHINGTON, October 20, 1917

DEAR MR. SECRETARY:

Confirming what I spoke to you about the other day, I really believe it would be serving efficiency and saving money if I could have an additional man in my office to do special work. As you know, Mr. Howe is wholly occupied now with new duties, such as expediting materials, procuring labor, etc. Two particular fields are now not being sufficiently covered. First,

I think we ought to check up all along the line to see whether we are not employing too many people in the hundreds of outside offices. For instance, we have employed hundreds of additional clerks and messengers in the navy yards, recruiting offices, naval district offices, etc., etc., and I get a good many tips from time to time that they are not all necessary. I cannot personally investigate a matter of this kind. Secondly, there is really need for checking up on the Naval Reserve and Militia. You and I have heard frequently of outlying districts where men are sitting around twiddling their thumbs and doing no real duty, etc. We also get many complaints about conditions in localities. My idea is that if we could get one man to look after these two loose ends he would save his pay many times over. I have thought of Livingston Davis, whom you know. He has good business experience, and at the same time has done practical Y.M.C.A. work, and has the kind of broad sympathy that would make him an excellent person to send anywhere if we wanted an investigation of conditions like, for instance, the Newport case. Furthermore, he is not the kind that would antagonize the naval officers.

I telephoned to Davis, and he says he would be delighted to come, but would have to be paid something. We have plenty of funds out of the Presidential allotment and, while this only runs to January 1st, some provision will have to be made for its continuance, because we are already employing many people out of it whom we cannot discharge on that date. I think Davis would come for, say, $3,000 per annum, and he could be called Special Assistant, or anything else you suggest.

F.D.R.

Approved by Mr. Daniels today Oct. 20

F. D. ROOSEVELT

WASHINGTON, October 29, 1917

MEMORANDUM FOR THE SECRETARY

Subject: Proposed measures to close English Channel and North Sea against submarines by mine barrage.

1. This is, of course, nothing more nor less than a resurrection of my proposition, which, with all earnestness possible, I called to the attention of the President, the Secretary of the Navy, the Chief of Operations, the General Board, Admiral Sims (and through him the British Admiralty), Admiral de Chair (and through him also the British Admiralty) and Admiral Chocheprat (and through him the French Ministry of Marine) during the months of May and June past.

2. While I have never claimed that the proposed plan was an infallible one, and while, quite properly, I have never attempted to lay down the exact location or the exact type of mines, etc., to be used in the barrage, I did state, and still state, that every consideration of common sense requires that the attempt be made, first in the English Channel and then in the North Sea.

3. But above all, starting when the Balfour and Viviani Missions were here in May, I reiterated the need for haste. I know how unseemly it is to seem to say "I told you so," but it is a literal fact that, while the British Admiralty may be blamed in part, our own Navy Department is at least largely responsible for failing to consider this proposition seriously during all of these months—May, June, July, August, September and October—which have gone over the dam beyond recall.

4. Now, this is the milk in the cocoanut: The powers that be seem at last willing to take up this proposition seriously. Unless we are willing to throw up our hands and say it is too late, we must admit that the same need for immediate haste

exists today as existed last May. We have done altogether too
much amiable "consideration" of this matter. If it is to be carried out at all it must be carried out with a different spirit from
any of the operations up to now. It will require prompt decision all along the line and an immediate carrying out of the
procurement of the material—mines and ships.

5. To accomplish the above it should be placed in the hands
of one man on our part and one man on the part of the British.
These two men should receive orders from their governments,
not as to details, but simply orders to carry out the plan. *And
most important of all, these men should have all the authority
requisite to do this.* This is a bigger matter than sending destroyers abroad or a division of battleships, or building a bunch
of new destroyers—it is vital to the winning of the war. Its success cannot be guaranteed. No military or naval operation can
be guaranteed. But if it works it will be the biggest single fac-
tor in winning the war. I have seen something during the past
four and a half years of how our present Navy Department
organization works and it so happens that I am also fairly familiar with the way the British Admiralty works. If the suggested plan is carried out solely under the present organizations
its chance of success will, in my judgment, be seriously dimin-
ished. You need somebody with imagination and authority to
make the try.

6. I know you will not mind my sending a copy of this to
the President, as I have discussed it with him several times.

FRANKLIN D. ROOSEVELT

[Admiral Dudley S. deChair was British naval representative
in Washington and Vice Admiral Paul Chocheprat was the
French naval representative. Lord Balfour was the British For-

eign Minister from 1917 to 1919, having previously served as
First Lord of the Admiralty. René Viviani, former Premier and
Foreign Minister of France, was Minister of Justice in the
Briand cabinet in 1917.]

Roosevelt confesses in the above memorandum that it is
"unseemly" for him to say "I told you so." The fact that his
position proved to be the correct one hardly makes the memorandum any less "unseemly," particularly since Wilson and
Daniels both supported the proposal. Besides lecturing the Secretary, Roosevelt sent the memorandum directly to the President, an unusual procedure for an Assistant Secretary. That
F.D.R. knew he was going too far is made clear in a letter to
his wife on the same day the memorandum was completed. He
wrote her that he had "given the Sec'y a very stinging memorandum and sent a copy to the President. Some day they will
be interesting reading." [7]

Well before the United States entered the war, Wilson often
asked Daniels why the British did not adopt the convoy system
for merchant ships, which had been successfully employed for
troop transports, and why the British did not place a barrage
in the North Sea to keep the U-boats in home ports. "Daniels,
why don't the British shut up the hornets in their nests," the
President said more than once. [8]

In 1916 Roosevelt sent Wilson a paper proposing a mine
barrage in the North Sea and in the English Channel. But both
the British and American navies thought the convoy and the
mine barrage too expensive and too cumbersome to be effective.

As U-boat sinkings increased, however, the British finally, in

7. F. D. R., *His Personal Letters, 1905-1928,* ed. Elliott Roosevelt (New
York, Duell, Sloan and Pearce, 1948), p. 363.

8. Josephus Daniels, *The Wilson Era, Years of War and After* (Chapel
Hill, The University of North Carolina Press, 1946), p. 83.

the summer of 1917, were forced to convoy merchant vessels on their homeward voyages and later on the outward voyages as well.

"The convoy system will ever stand as a monument to the constancy and courage of the Royal Navy and Mercantile Marine," Winston Churchill said after the war. "No service ever carried out by the Navy was of greater value to the State than that of the escort vessels.... The mine however proved to be the most effective killing weapon." [9]

But the mine was not employed so soon as the convoy. Two or three attempts to make use of mine fields in the war against the submarine had been unsuccessful, thus confirming the critics of the mine in their belief in its ineffectiveness. On April 16, 1917, Daniels cabled Admiral William S. Sims, the American naval representative in London: "Is it not practicable to blockade German coast efficiently and completely, thus making practically impossible the egress and ingress of submarines?" Two days later Sims replied that the plan was "quite unfeasible."

By the end of 1917, however, an extensive mine field was tried out in the Dover area and proved successful. In 1918 a vast mine field, across 180 miles of water, was laid between Norway and the Orkney Islands by the British and American navies. After the war, Daniels wrote: "Not laying that barrage earlier—in fact, at the earliest possible moment—was, in my opinion, the greatest naval error of the war." [10]

Rear Admiral Frederic R. Harris, chief of the Bureau of Yards and Docks from 1915 to 1917 and one of those who took a leading part in working out the mine-laying scheme, gave much of the credit to Roosevelt, but in his book *Our Navy at War* Daniels makes no reference to

9. Winston Churchill, *The World Crisis 1916-1918* (New York, Charles Scribner's Sons, 1927), II, 83, 84.
10. Daniels, *Our Navy at War*, p. 130.

Roosevelt in discussing the mine controversy. Later, however, in *The Wilson Era—Years of War and After*, Daniels wrote that among those who early shared Wilson's belief "that U-boats should and could be shut up in German waters were Secretary of Commerce Redfield and Assistant Secretary of the Navy Franklin Roosevelt. They communicated their opinions to Wilson, and Roosevelt took up with him plans that had been drawn in the Navy Department." [11] Harris was quoted as saying, "If Roosevelt had not been there the North Sea Barrage would never have been laid down, in my opinion. Certainly my own interest in it was due to his enthusiasm and encouragement." [12]

WASHINGTON, April 5, 1918

MY DEAR MR. DANIELS:

Following our several talks recently, and as you suggest, I am putting down a rough list of the various activities of the Navy on the other side. As you know, most of the requisitions for materials, and you might say the business and legal part of the Naval operations in Europe, come over my desk. Their volume has assumed such proportions and such a diversity that it is next to impossible for those over here without a close knowledge of affairs over there to form an intelligent opinion upon which to base appropriate action. All the Navy shore stations, whether in Ireland, England, France or Gibraltar, are theoretically under Admiral Sims, and the cables in regard to these stations are reaching a very large daily total. It is obvious from an inspection of these daily cables that while of course Admiral Sims has been

---

11. Daniels, *The Wilson Era—Years of War and After*, pp. 83-84.
12. Ernest K. Lindley, *Franklin D. Roosevelt, a Career in Progressive Democracy* (Indianapolis, The Bobbs-Merrill Company, 1931), p. 160.

magnificent in the way he has handled the work, it would be a great help to him to have me go over there for a short time to help him coordinate the business end of his work. Admiral Benson entirely approves, and Admiral Sims himself has written that he would be only too glad if I could go over.

I hesitate to speak about the personal side of it, but many of the returning officers have been good enough to say that it would help our Naval officers and men on the other side if I could look in on them and see their work at first hand.

But aside from this I feel the business efficiency of the forces and especially of the shore stations could be benefited and there have been a good many cases in the cables of late that made me feel that things could be improved from the administrative standpoint.

If the President approves, there is no particular reason why I could not go now just as well as later. I could perfectly well catch the cruiser that leaves on Sunday.

Very sincerely yours,

FRANKLIN D. ROOSEVELT

[Admiral William S. Benson was Chief of Naval Operations.]

Permission was not immediately granted for Roosevelt to leave Washington. He did not sail on "the cruiser that leaves on Sunday." He left, instead, on the destroyer, U.S.S. *Dyer*, on July 9, with Captain Edward McCauley as his aide and Marine Sergeant W. W. Stratton as his orderly. The *Dyer* reached the Azores July 15 and Portsmouth, England, July 21. In England, Roosevelt conferred with Sir Eric Geddes, First Lord of the Admiralty, and other officials. He left on

July 31, arriving in Paris for conferences with French states-
men on August 1. On August 7 he went to Rome for more
conferences. He returned to England the end of August for
a visit with the Grand Fleet. On September 12 he sailed
from Brest aboard the U.S.S. *Leviathan*, arriving in New
York a week later.

U.S.S. *Dyer* AT SEA, July 18, 1918

MY DEAR MR. DANIELS:

We have had a most successful trip so far and have completed our visit in the Azores. The wind has been very astern
all the way and I have been lucky enough to feel entirely
well.

On Monday we spent 5 hours at Horta, the principal town
of the Island of Fayal. I went ashore and was somewhat
horrified to find that there is not a single American on the
island, the Consular agent, a Portuguese, having been removed
by the State Department some months ago. This is the only
harbour in the Azores, except our Naval Base at Ponta del
Gada and is 160 miles nearer the American Coast.

We arrived at Ponta del Gada on Tuesday morning. Was
met by Admiral Dunn; General Machado, the Portuguese
High Commissioner, who is a sort of Governor-general over
the island; Admiral Newparth, the Portuguese Admiral, who
has two small ships under him but expects a third.

We have there a gun-boat with a cracked shaft. Two old
yachts which cannot go to sea and a sailing ship full of oil.
On shore we have a Flying Detachment of the Marine Corps
and four old type planes, of which only two can occasionally
get off the water, also two 7″ guns. One mounted to protect
the harbour and the other a few miles down the coast to
protect the radio station....

In regard to the Naval situation, Azores will necessarily become a port of call to a very great extent, during the coming year, for our new destroyers, Eagle boats, etc. For instance, the day after I left, Admiral Dunn was expecting 35 Navy ships on the way from the United States, 25 110-footers and 10 larger vessels. . . .

I hope that all goes well. I will write you when I get to London. This has been a most wonderful trip and a real rest in spite of the destroyer.

Give my love to everybody.

Faithfully yours,
FRANKLIN D. ROOSEVELT

[Rear Admiral Herbert Omar Dunn commanded the American naval base in the Azores in 1918-1919.]

LONDON, July 29, 1918

MY DEAR MR. DANIELS:

I have had a busy three days in London and am leaving tomorrow morning for Dover, Dunkirk and Paris.

I have been at the Admiralty several times and this morning went to see the King and had a very pleasant forty minutes' talk with him. He was very complimentary about our Naval forces over here and the earnest spirit of cooperation which is apparent everywhere. He also spoke a good deal about the outrages committed by the Germans in their retirement from Chateau Thierry, and gave me many instances which prove that the destruction of property and the outrages against women are without question under direct orders of the higher German command. The whole thing has been too systematic to assume it to be the action of the individual soldiery. Also I have talked with a good many of our own Army people here, and they are very insistent on the feeling among the men of our own forces that a drastic lesson against the Germans themselves on German soil will be necessary before any understanding can be hammered into the German mind....

I will write you from Paris after we have seen the Flying Base at Dunkirk. That particular point is under constant shell fire and we shall have an interesting trip.

Always sincerely yours,

FRANKLIN D. ROOSEVELT

EN ROUTE TO PARIS, August 2, 1918

MY DEAR MR. DANIELS:

Before leaving London on Tuesday, I lunched at the Embassy and had a most delightful talk with Mr. Lloyd George. I know you would enjoy meeting him. He strikes one immediately as a great leader of men. One of the things that has struck me particularly this week in England has been the absolute unanimity among all the Government people here to see this thing through to more than what they call "a patched-up peace."

I also had another talk with Mr. Balfour and with Sir Eric Geddes about the Mediterranean situation....

On Wednesday morning we were at Dover, where we saw Admiral Keyes and went into the question of the Channel defenses and patrol. I am a little amused by the fact that they are carrying out certain operations now, which you will remember I tried to have taken up for weeks and months in the Spring and Summer of 1917. As a result, the English Channel is now fairly successfully blocked against submarines and only one, or possibly two, have got through in several months. The plans which are now being carried out ought to make the Channel wholly closed.

We crossed over to Dunkirk on a British destroyer, seeing a great fleet of French fishing boats as we neared the French coast. This additional food supply is one of the results of the present safety of things in the Channel. . . .

Just got to Paris—All well.

Faithfully yours,
FRANKLIN D. ROOSEVELT

[David Lloyd George was the British Prime Minister. Admiral Sir Roger J. B. Keyes commanded the Dover Patrol.]

WASHINGTON, 5 August 1918

TELEGRAM TO ROOSEVELT IN PARIS

Letter from Azores received and suggestions will be carried out where possible. Glad you are going to Rome. Happy over your message about splendid fighting of our troops. Get all information about the fighting of marines with any special instances of more than usual courage. Destroyer builders working better and every energy employed for speeding up work on them. The whole country cheered by news from the front. . . .

JOSEPHUS DANIELS

PARIS, August 13, 1918

MY DEAR MR. DANIELS:

I am back in Paris again for a few hours after a very successful visit of three days in Rome. It was a flying visit, but well worth the long trip. . . .

Italy itself seems to be in much better shape than a few months ago. Our Red Cross has done splendid work, also

Professor Merriam, of the Committee on Public Information. I held a reception for the newspaper men of Rome and the representatives of the Italian Press Associations. Of course, Italy is not in the war in the same sense that France and England are, and they feel a little bit out of it so far as help from the United States and others is concerned. We cannot expect them to make the same sacrifices as France and England have made, and while some of their demands may be a little unreasonable I think we should stretch a point and give them as much help as we possibly can....

I hope all goes well with you. Quantities of people have begged me to get you over here in the Fall. You really ought to decide to come in October and you could get back again by the time Congress reopens.

Always faithfully yours,
FRANKLIN D. ROOSEVELT

[Professor Charles Edward Merriam of the University of Chicago was a member of the Committee on Public Information in Italy.]

PARIS, August 25, 1918

TELEGRAM TO DANIELS

Have completed inspection west coast ports. Conditions on the whole excellent and relations with French Navy entirely satisfactory. Have also visited Belgian front and Belgian King. Am leaving Paris for London Tuesday, thence to Grand Fleet and east coast bases, hoping to sail for home about September fifth.

ROOSEVELT

[Roosevelt sailed on September 12.]

LONDON, Sept. 4, 1918

PRIVATE FOR THE SECRETARY:

For your own information only, I have long thought of my proper duty in the war and now after organization work is nearly completed I am certain I should be in active service in some capacity. Army has asked me to consider work in France but in view of long association I naturally prefer Navy if possible and therefore will ask you about October first for a commission in Navy or Marines that will insure service at front. I do not need to tell you how hard it will be for me to end our work together, but know you will understand.

ROOSEVELT

Roosevelt told Daniels early in the war that he wished to get into active service. When Daniels urged him to continue his work as Assistant Secretary, Roosevelt, who was thirty-five in 1917, went to see the President. Wilson told him that he was rendering a greater service in the Navy Department and refused to accept his resignation. "Around the Department," Daniels wrote later, "it was said that, inasmuch as his cousin Theodore left the position of Assistant Secretary to become a Rough Rider, later Governor of New York and then President, and both had served in the Legislature of New York, Franklin thought actual fighting in the war was the necessary step toward reaching the White House." [13]

Shortly after Roosevelt renewed his request from London in September, 1918, he became seriously ill with pneumonia and it was mid-October before he was able to return to Washington. He then became ill with the flu. When he regained his strength, he went to see the President to press

13. Daniels, *The Wilson Era, Years of Peace*, p. 130.

his request for active service. The President informed him that the Armistice was near.

On October 1, 1918, Roosevelt wrote a long report on his European inspection trip. On the question of the North Sea barrage, he said:

"As you know, this has been what might be called my pet hobby since the inception of the war. You will remember that I pushed this matter as early as May, 1917; that after some time the Bureau of Ordnance indorsed the principle and worked out what it considered practicable plans. In the meanwhile, I had, with your knowledge, taken the matter up with the British and French Admiralties and with Mr. Balfour. The French Navy indorsed the proposition in principle, but the British Admiralty at that time considered it impracticable. Finally, three or four months later, the plan was officially put forward by the Division of Operations, although Admiral Benson said quite frankly that he did not personally believe in its practicability. It was accepted, however, by the British Admiralty in the autumn of 1917, they undertaking to lay the English Channel Barrage, and we undertaking to lay the major part of the North Sea Barrage. This operation has been conducted under the command of Admiral Strauss, and is proceeding on the whole very satisfactorily. This is the opinion of Admiral Sims and he is whole-heartedly in favor of the completion of this North Sea Barrage. The British Admiralty stands committed to it, but Admiral Sir David Beatty, Commanding the Grand Fleet south of the barrage line, has from the beginning shown little enthusiasm, and has in fact insisted on various modifications of channels through the barrage. Admiral Sims has insisted that the barrage be made complete, i.e., from land to land without gaps. I believe and recommend that the Navy Department should back up Admiral Sims to the limit in this matter."

Rear Admiral Joseph Strauss, who had been Chief of the

Bureau of Ordnance, was in charge of the Mine Barrage Force that in 1918 planted 56,000 American mines in the North Sea. In 1919, Strauss commanded the American forces that cleared the North Sea of these same mines.

On November 11, the Armistice was finally signed, and the Navy was faced with the difficult task of demobilizing its forces and settling its large business affairs in Europe. Roosevelt was primarily responsible for these business matters and promptly asked to be sent to Europe to handle them on the spot.

WASHINGTON, 14 November 1918

DEAR MR. DANIELS:

In regard to the dispatches from Sims and Benson regarding the demobilization of Naval Forces in European waters, on which immediate action is asked, may I call your attention to the report which I made to you on returning from Europe.

I did not criticize what might be called the business end of our work there because of the necessity at that time of thinking of the work of actual operations, but I did call attention to the fact that an enormous number of contracts, claims, both personal and property, readjustments, etc., etc., had been laid on one side pending the termination of hostilities.

I recommended then that an Assistant Secretary be sent over *at that time* to undertake immediately the settling of these business questions. If there was necessity then for this action, there is greater necessity now.

Furthermore, I told you that in my judgment the business work on shore was too much scattered in the hands of young officers without great experience.

We are face to face with this problem today. The demobilization can and should begin at once.

Are you going to leave it solely in the hands of Admiral Sims and the Naval Officers who have built it up?

I am absolutely certain that a civilian is needed in charge of this demobilization because it is not merely a matter of packing up material and sending the men home. The dealings will be almost wholly with other civilians of England, France and Italy,—not with naval officers.

I, therefore, again suggest that an Assistant Secretary be sent abroad immediately and given complete authority to deal with the disposal of property and the settling of the Navy's financial relations with the Foreign Governments and their citizens.

This civilian does not need a large staff. He should have, however, one or possibly two good lawyers, one first-class Paymaster, and one first-class Civil Engineer. The rest of the organization can be created from the Naval Forces now in Europe. The work must be undertaken in conjunction with the Army and the Army already has a staff organized for it.

Very sincerely yours,

FRANKLIN D. ROOSEVELT

WASHINGTON, 21 November 1918

MY DEAR MR. DANIELS:

How can one correct a policy telegram if the policy itself is wrong?

The first part of this dispatch deals with generalities; the second part goes into too much detail as to what should be returned and what should be disposed of, and the whole shows the utter fallacy of trying to conduct the demobilization in Europe from the Navy Department in Washington.

The crux of the whole matter is this—Are you going to let the Navy people on the other side handle this business matter with their present officers, or are you going to put it in the hands of business people?

I have been abroad and have seen things with my own eyes, and I want to repeat again what I said in my report on my return and in my letter to you of last week, that there is so much involved in this demobilization—millions of dollars of materials, contracts, claims, assets, liabilities, and even more important international relations with foreign governments and foreign citizens that I must protest definitely and vigorously against its being handled by the existing Navy organization in Europe.

You know that I have just as high a regard for Sims, Tobey, and the other officers as you have. They have proved their ability to build up and operate the Navy machine for war purposes. And you know as I do that the training of these officers, Line or Staff, does not fit them for what is nine tenths a civilian job, the disposal of material, the settling of thousands of legal questions, and the handling of these matters with French, English and Italian civilian officials.

No Paymaster that you can send over has enough rank or authority to act as American Commissioner in collaboration with English and French Cabinet Officers.

I must respectfully recommend, as I have before, that the only way to handle this is to send over a Commissioner with the rank of Assistant Secretary, to give him adequate legal assistance, and to give him above all full authority to speak for the Navy and to settle matters in close cooperation with our Army once and for all.

You can give him general instructions as an outline of your

policy, but to tell him here, for instance, that he should ship home all automobiles is ridiculous. How can we tell in Washington as to whether it would be better to send some automobiles home or sell them on the other side?

I feel so strongly about this, because of my knowledge of the situation, that I have put my views in this letter in a way which is perhaps too strong. The reason I do so is because I want your administration of the Navy to continue without scandal or criticism, and, equally, I want to see our Navy take its final departure from Europe with the continued goodwill and appreciation of the people and the governments of France, Great Britain and Italy.

Very sincerely yours,

FRANKLIN D. ROOSEVELT

WASHINGTON, Dec. 4, 1918

DEAR ROOSEVELT:

I am sorry to know that your throat is giving you trouble again and hope it is slight and you will soon be out.

The question of what to do about contracts and materials in Europe has given me great concern, but in view of the necessity of securing and explaining the legislation needed and the use of sums already granted and disposing of the many ships and yachts and other material on this side of the water, I have reached the conclusion that both [of] us must stay in Washington until March fourth. The business across is important, but that here at home will require the united work and effort of both of us to readjust and to secure the necessary legislation. This conclusion has been forced upon me by the multitude of big things we must take up here. I wish you to go into the matter of all the ships leased and purchased so that we may turn them back at the least expense possible....

Sincerely yours,

JOSEPHUS DANIELS

WASHINGTON, Dec. 7, 1918

[In longhand.]

DEAR MR. DANIELS:

I am still laid up in the house and doubt if I shall get down to the office until Monday—hence I am writing about a matter in which time is an essential, and which is to me very important.

I understand perfectly what you say in your note about the importance of the work to be done here, and I am of course glad that you think I can be of help.

But I fear very much that you have still left unanswered the equally important question of the financial and legal side of naval demobilization in Europe. In other words, the question has never been whether *I* should go abroad—or whether *I* could be more useful to you here or there—as I told you somewhat emphatically the other day it is quite immaterial to me whether *I* go or not.

But, frankly, it is not immaterial to me to see my recommendations to you wholly disregarded and an inefficient and dangerous state of affairs continued....

Twice since October 15th I have in the absence of any action begged you again in writing to send someone over to superintend and to centralize this work. And finally two weeks ago you and I discussed the subject and you agreed with me that the plans worked up by the Bureaus and by the Division of Operations were wrong in principle.

Nevertheless, the very next day, Nov. 23, you approved this operations plan and cabled it to Sims. Then two days later you agreed with me that it should be immediately changed, and I told you of the need for haste, because settlements and sales would soon be made on the other side under the piecemeal, local, hit or miss method already approved.

May I emphasize again that in all of this I have never once recommended that you send me or any other particular individual. The sole issue is the settling of our Navy business and legal matters in Europe to the credit of the Navy and of the Government.

This matter is in my judgment so vital, and is one with which I am personally so familiar that in it I must keep my own record clear. Therefore I must with the greatest respect insist either on appropriate action being taken, or on my position being made so clear to the public that I may never be considered to have acquiesced in what I feel to be a failure to handle the problem rightly.

Very sincerely yours,

FRANKLIN D. ROOSEVELT

WASHINGTON, Dec. 7, 1918

DEAR ROOSEVELT:

Of course it would be much better if one of us could go over, but as that is impossible owing to the pressing duties here, we must arrange the next best plan. Our experience has been that our men in the service handle these matters better than civilians called from private life.

I hope you will be all right on Monday and will talk over and consider the best arrangements.

Sincerely,

JOSEPHUS DANIELS

Daniels finally acquiesced under Roosevelt's persistent pressure. An undated pencilled note by Roosevelt to Admiral Benson says: "Assistant Secretary of the Navy will leave for London Dec. 15 and will be in full charge of all questions in Europe involving disposal of all navy property, etc." Daniels did not sign Roosevelt's travel orders, however, until December 24, when he gave F.D.R. "full authority to ascertain the status of all outstanding contracts.... and to settle such obligations incurred by the Navy and claims arising from Naval operations abroad." Roosevelt sailed from New York on January 2, 1919.

NEW YORK, January 2, 1919

TELEGRAM TO DANIELS

Sailed this morning. All well. Please advise me when personnel are landed from U.S.S. *Northern Pacific*, also any other important Navy information. Good wishes to you all.

ROOSEVELT

WASHINGTON, January 7, 1919

TELEGRAM TO ROOSEVELT ON BOARD U.S.S. *George Washington*

My wife joins me in sincere sympathy to you and Mrs. Roosevelt. The death of ex-President Roosevelt came as a shock to the whole country.

JOSEPHUS DANIELS

[Former President Theodore Roosevelt died unexpectedly on January 6, 1919.]

PARIS, January 1919

TELEGRAM TO DANIELS

Saw Josephus at Brest. He never looked better but he is keen to get home. I see no reason why he should not do so now as he has had excellent experience and other officers are returning. Unless you object I will arrange it from this end.

ROOSEVELT

[Josephus Daniels, Jr., was a lieutenant in the Marine Corps.]

WASHINGTON, January 1919

TELEGRAM TO ROOSEVELT

Under new conditions I am forced to decline many applications for release and think he should not return just now. We are keen to see him and I am writing him today. No action should be taken until he receives my letter.

JOSEPHUS DANIELS

LONDON, 28 January, 1919

MY DEAR MR. DANIELS:

We have been here in London for a week and things are working out well in every respect. The five days in France were valuable because I was able to get in touch with Admiral Benson before he left for the Conference at Treves. . . .

The most successful thing I pulled off in Paris was the sale of the radio station to the French Government. They had backed and filled for over six weeks, and I finally put it up to Tardieu and told him that if they did not wish to keep the LaFayette Station themselves, I would have to take the material down and ship it home for use at the new Monroe station. They agreed to take it the next day. . . .

Over here in England, the number of stations is not as large, but the amounts involved are pretty heavy. I found that our Army people had entered into a perfectly wild agree-

ment with the British Air Ministry. Their agreement is very
loosely drawn and in my judgment will mean negotiations
carried on for several years to come. . . .

I go from here to Brussels on Sunday to talk over some
of the operations of the Northern Bombing Squadron. We
will get back to Paris on February 6th, and eight or ten days
work there will clean up the whole situation as far as it is
possible to do so at this time. Therefore, I expect to sail for
home February 15th. . . .

Faithfully,
FRANKLIN D. ROOSEVELT

[André Tardieu was special French representative in the
United States during the last years of the war and a member
of the Peace Conference.]

In his annual report for 1919, Daniels wrote: "Upon the
signing of the Armistice and the closing of Naval shore
activities abroad, the Navy had a number of stations in
Europe, and valuable material and equipment. In order that
it might be sold, salvaged or brought to America, as in each
case was most desirable, Assistant Secretary Roosevelt, accompanied by Commander John M. Hancock, who had
shown high ability in the business side of the Navy in
cooperation with the War Industries Board, and Mr. Thomas
J. Spellacy, an able lawyer, as legal adviser, went to Europe
in January and made arrangements by which the Navy's
demobilization could be expedited and its property disposed
of to the best advantage.

"The plans perfected and the negotiations completed have
resulted in the disposition of Naval property in a way that
has been wise and beneficial. The great high-power radio
station in France was, through negotiations with the French

Government, completed by our Navy, with the agreement that it be purchased by the French Government. Equipment and material that will be needed at home have been brought back and such as was not practicable or profitable to transport has been sold abroad."

John M. Hancock, who accompanied Roosevelt to Europe, was in charge of Navy purchasing from 1914 to 1919 and later was a prominent industrial banker. In a letter to this writer, Mr. Hancock said: "I can say that I have a very high appreciation of Mr. Daniels and that I think a great deal of the progress the Navy made during his time was due to his wisdom. Unhappily, his relations with the Service people generally were not such as to induce wholehearted support from the Service."

U.S.S. *George Washington*, AT SEA,

Feb. 21, 1919

MY DEAR MR. DANIELS:

I am taking this opportunity, on the voyage home, of giving you a summary of the work accomplished for the demobilization of the U. S. Naval Forces in Europe. As you will remember, I pointed out to you last autumn the great variety of naval enterprises undertaken across the ocean, the large number of shore stations and of ships, the thousands of personnel and the importance of the financial obligations involved in carrying out the work; and I recommended that you send a representative clothed with authority to expedite the demobilization and to settle all matters pertaining to Navy business.

You gave me this authority and I sailed from New York on this ship on January 1st [2nd].... Briefly stated, the work of the Navy in Europe has been excellently and expeditiously handled. During the war it was of course necessary to take

over property by commandeering, by the assistance of foreign
and local governing bodies and sometimes by direct means
without going through Government channels. The Navy had
54 bases and stations widely scattered in the different European countries, not including 25 or more Port Offices, head-
quarters, etc. Excellent progress was made between November 11th and my arrival in January in settling the claims,
contracts, etc., and in closing the stations, but it was of value,
I believe, to have one person in whom authority was central-
ized and I was able to close up all of the larger cases. . . .

FRANKLIN D. ROOSEVELT

Roosevelt's disagreements with Daniels while they were
in the Navy Department together were many. But after the
first few months Roosevelt's patronizing comments ceased,
and he stopped making fun of Daniels' manners. His respect
for his Chief increased, particularly as he recognized Daniels'
courage, liberalism, and political capacity. In dedicating the
second volume of *F.D.R., His Personal Letters* "to the memory of two great Americans, Josephus Daniels and Louis
McHenry Howe," Elliott Roosevelt said that they "should
justly be credited with developing in Franklin D. Roosevelt
a maturity and an outlook which might easily not have
existed without their influence." In a Foreword to the volume, Eleanor Roosevelt said that at times her husband was
critical of Daniels, "but he learned as time went on to have
a deep admiration for the qualities of character and to value
the high ability of Mr. Daniels." F.D.R. particularly benefited from watching Daniels push one Navy bill through
Congress after another. "It was his own experience," Mrs.
Roosevelt said, "that taught him it was one thing to understand and get on with naval officers, and another and perhaps

even greater quality that enabled Mr. Daniels to understand and get on with Congress. What he spoke of slightly at first, he came to admire inordinately because of all the difficulties he himself encountered." [14]

Daniels' critics were many during his eight years in the Cabinet. But Wilson always supported and defended him. Wilson's son-in-law and Secretary of the Treasury likewise resented the ridicule often levelled at Daniels. In his autobiography, McAdoo wrote: "The Navy went through the World War under Daniels' direction; it has never been, at any period of its history, more efficient, yet its excellent record did not silence Daniels' critics. The President used to say that the vilification of Daniels emanated wholly, he thought, from disappointed contractors who found the stream of easy money dried up when Daniels was put in charge of the department." [15]

Daniels, of course, gave the editorialists, the cartoonists, and the naval officers many chances to take shots at him by his prohibition orders, his order to use "right" and "left" in place of "port" and "starboard" (an order signed by F.D.R.), and his general disregard for Navy tradition, particularly when he thought the old rules and practices were not democratic.

WASHINGTON, April 3, 1919

DEAR MR. DANIELS:

Ever since you left, things have been so quiet here as to be almost terrifying. Literally nothing has happened outside of the routine work, which, however, has been positively voluminous, and all I can say is that I have the deepest

14. F. D. R., *His Personal Letters, 1905-1928*, ed. Elliott Roosevelt (New York, Duell, Sloan and Pearce, 1948), p. xviii.

15. William G. McAdoo, *Crowded Years* (Boston and New York, Houghton, Mifflin Company, 1931), p. 185.

sympathy for what happened to you when I was away on both of my trips to Europe. I am awfully glad that the trip over was so successful and that you had a good rest. We have followed your visit to Paris and the Chateau Thierry front with the greatest interest, and now you are off for Italy.

We have given some good hand-outs to the press on various items which you knew about, and McIntyre and Jenkins are on the job, doing well.

Your family are apparently in splendid health, and the only catastrophe was a slight accident to your car, which, however, has since been mended and put in operation again.

The only thing which has rather appalled me, and which I have only just heard of today, is the appointment of Captain R. H. Jackson to command the Base at the Azores, in the place of Admiral Dunn. Frankly, I am rather upset, because I saw Jackson in Paris, on my first trip, and he is decidedly the last man in the world to send to a place like the Azores, or to any other spot where tact and good manners are desirable. I know very well that he is a protege of Admiral Benson, but I consider I am a better judge of Jackson's qualities in his relations with foreigners than Benson can ever hope to be. He was taken out of the Paris post on my recommendation, as you know, but was kept there for two months thereafter by some strange piece of work which I have never been able to fathom. Now he gets a very important post, for which he is disqualified for the same reasons that removed him from Paris. R. H. Jackson may be a good officer in command of a ship—that I do not know anything about—but I cannot help feeling, in view of my knowledge of the case, often expressed, that he should be relieved from the Azores and sent somewhere else immediately.

My wife joins me in warmest regards to you both. We are, at the present moment, suffering from intense cold, in fact the last week has been far more like winter than the first three weeks of March.

Always sincerely yours,
FRANKLIN D. ROOSEVELT

[Daniels went to Europe in mid-March, 1919, to attend the Naval Conference. He returned to Washington on May 18. Marvin McIntyre and John Wilber Jenkins were the Navy press officers. McIntyre later became secretary to the President when F.D.R. entered the White House. Rear Admiral Dunn was in command of the naval base in the Azores.]

ON BATTLESHIP New York, August 31, 1919

DEAR FRANKLIN:

We are coming in to Monterey and will reach San Francisco Sunday night ready for the review on Labor Day.... We had truly a glorious time in Honolulu and at Hilo.... I feel somewhat like a shirker to be away so long, but feel that it is important while on the West Coast to finish the inspection and study for it will be a live and important matter in the next and succeeding Congresses.

My wife sends her love to Mrs. Roosevelt. This is an idyllic trip and you should both look forward to it as a second honeymoon trip. Remember us to all at the Department.

Sincerely, with warm regards,
JOSEPHUS DANIELS

[Daniels visited the Hawaiian Islands in August, 1919, on a Navy inspection trip.]

WASHINGTON, 10 September, 1919

MEMORANDUM FOR MR. DANIELS

The enclosed letter from Admiral Knapp is merely the type you will get from nine out of ten of the senior officers of the Navy, admirals or captains.

As usual you will find that they don't like the Selection Board but are horribly scared of any different form of legislation which will prevent promotion by seniority.

As you know, they were opposed to the Selection Board until they found that it worked out without doing anybody any harm except the efficiency of the service. As long as the selection board picks the top men on the lists the older officers will be for it and opposed to any change.

F. D. ROOSEVELT

[Vice Admiral H. S. Knapp commanded U. S. Naval forces in European waters, succeeding Admiral Sims in March, 1919.]

There was little correspondence between the Secretary and the Assistant Secretary during the next few months. Roosevelt and Daniels were interested in political developments, but there were many business matters to keep them busy in the Navy Department. In June, 1920, the Republicans met in Chicago and on the tenth ballot nominated Senator Warren G. Harding of Ohio as their presidential candidate and Governor Calvin Coolidge of Massachusetts as their vice presidential candidate. The Democrats then met in San Francisco and after another lengthy party battle, reminiscent of the long fight to nominate Wilson at the Baltimore convention of 1912, finally nominated Governor James M. Cox of Ohio on the forty-fourth ballot. He was a compromise candidate. On July 6, with the approval of Cox, F.D.R. was nominated as his running mate. When the delegates demanded that Roosevelt make a speech, he left the auditorium rather than break precedent and speak before his formal notification. Daniels pinch-hit and made the speech for Roosevelt.

On August 3, 1920, Daniels received a formal invitation from the Democratic National Committee to attend the ceremonies at Hyde Park August 9 notifying F.D.R. of his nomination as Vice President.

4

WASHINGTON, July 26, 1920

TELEGRAM TO DANIELS IN YELLOWSTONE PARK, WYOMING

My notification set for August ninth. Am therefore submitting my resignation to President to take effect that day. I need not tell you of my sorrow that this step is necessary. In regard to successor think I have solution which will appeal to you. I leave for Eastport tonight and will be back here August third and stay till sixth. My wife and I sincerely hope you and Mrs. Daniels can come to Hyde Park for the notification.

ROOSEVELT

WASHINGTON, August 6th, 1920

[In longhand.]

MY DEAR CHIEF:

This is not goodbye—that will always be impossible after these years of the closest association—and no words I write will make you know better than you know now how much our association has meant. All my life I shall look back,—not only on the *work* of the place—but mostly on the wonderful way in which you and I have gone through these nearly eight years *together*. You have taught me so wisely and kept my feet on the ground when I was about to skyrocket—and in it all there has never been a real dispute or antagonism or distrust.

Hence, in part, at least, I will share in the reward which you *will* get true credit for in history. I am very proud—but more than that I am very *happy* to have been able to help.

We will I know keep up this association in the years to come—and please let me keep on coming to you to get your fine inspiration of real idealism and right living and good Americanism.

So *au revoir* for a little while. You have always the

Affectionate regards of

FRANKLIN D. ROOSEVELT

WASHINGTON, August 7, 1920

DEAR FRANKLIN:

Your words of sincere friendship were very grateful to me and I am happy to know that the years of service have strengthened the friendship which began, I think, upon our first acquaintance. Love at first sight is rare with men, but sometimes I flatter myself in believing that I have some of woman's intuition, and on the day the President asked me to become Secretary of the Navy, I told my wife I would recommend your appointment as Assistant Secretary if it was agreeable for you to be a co-worker in the Department. I was pleased to find that it was in line with your taste and congenial to your long interest in naval matters. And so, with mutual regard and mutual consecration, we have spent seven and a half years in the service of our country. We little thought then of the great responsibility we were assuming, but we were not of the type of men who run from work or seek to escape responsibility. I am happy that we were given the great job in the World War, and it will always be a matter of gratulation that the team work of naval direction resulted in such efficient contribution to victory.

I always counted on your zeal, your enthusiasm, your devoted patriotism and efficient and able service, and always found you equal to the big job in hand. My thought and feeling has been that of an older brother and your nomination to the great office of Vice President by our party pleased me very much, and I shall always rejoice in your successes and victories and be glad if in any way I can contribute to them. More intimately I shall share with you the happiness that [comes] to you in your beautiful home life and we will be brothers in all things that make for the good of our country.

My wife joins me in love to your wife and mother.

Faithfully your friend,
JOSEPHUS DANIELS

During the war Daniels wrote a number of personal letters to Mrs. Roosevelt telling her of her husband's letters from abroad, etc., always referring to him as Franklin. Mrs. Roosevelt replied with short and courteous letters, once thanking Daniels for word about "my dear Franklin." Most Daniels letters to F.D.R. in this period are addressed "Dear Mr. Roosevelt," but in January and February, 1920, there are some routine ones addressed "Dear Franklin."

2

FROM DEFEAT TO VICTORY

WASHINGTON, August 13, 1920
TELEGRAM TO ROOSEVELT IN SOUTH DAKOTA

You are hitting the bull's eye in every speech. Eastern papers are giving prominence to speeches and they are making a very great impression.

JOSEPHUS DANIELS

BILLINGS, MONT., August 17, 1920
MY DEAR MR. DANIELS:

It was awfully good of you to send me your kind telegram of August 14th. I am very glad to know that the people in the East are pleased with the truths I am telling the people of the West.

I find the sentiment out here greatly in favor of the immediate signing of the Treaty with Germany and the ratification of the League of Nations' Covenant....

Always sincerely yours,
FRANKLIN D. ROOSEVELT

WASHINGTON, August 26, 1920

TELEGRAM TO ROOSEVELT AT SALT LAKE CITY, UTAH

I have appointed Gordon Woodbury of New Hampshire, strongly endorsed by all our friends, as your successor. Hope you will be here next week so as to give him benefit of your experience and advice. Let me know when you will reach Washington as my wife and I are expecting you to stay with us.

JOSEPHUS DANIELS

CANTON, ILL., October 11, 1920

MY DEAR MR. DANIELS:

. . . Things are looking better all the time. You have been doing simply marvelous work.

Do not forget that we expect Mrs. Daniels and yourself at Hyde Park after the Army & Navy Football Game. I hope, however, that I will see you before that time in Washington. I hope to get down soon after Election Day.

Very sincerely yours,

FRANKLIN D. ROOSEVELT

P.S. I am still alive and going fairly strong, tho' my voice is that of a crow!

The election of 1920 was a Republican landslide. Harding defeated Cox by seven million votes and the Republicans won overwhelming majorities in both houses of Congress. It was a "return to normalcy" that was not unexpected but which nevertheless caused tremendous gloom in the Democratic camp. "We had a chance to gain the leadership of the world," lamented Woodrow Wilson, the sick and repudiated President. "We have lost it, and soon we shall be witnessing the tragedy of it all." It was the beginning of twelve lean years for the Democrats.

WASHINGTON, January 3, 1921

MY DEAR FRANKLIN:

Your telegram of Christmas greetings added to the cheer of the day. All the boys were at home spending our last Christmas in Washington, and the message from you recalled the long and pleasant association. I am writing to wish for you and your good wife and mother and all the little Roosevelts our best wishes for the New Year, congratulations upon the new association you have formed, and our very best wishes always....

Sincerely your friend,

JOSEPHUS DANIELS

Roosevelt on January 15, 1921, wrote a "Dear Chief" letter to Daniels on stationery of Emmet, Marvin & Roosevelt, Counsellors at Law. Grenville T. Emmet, Langdon P. Marvin and Franklin D. Roosevelt were partners, with offices at 52 Wall Street, New York.

In Washington, Daniels was winding up his eight years in the Navy Department, preparing to return to Raleigh in March to edit his *News and Observer*. But his boundless energy was more than the paper demanded and even before he left Washington he made plans to write a special series of syndicated newspaper articles. On February 22, Daniels wrote to Roosevelt asking for his recollection of certain war-time events, and Roosevelt replied:

NEW YORK, February 25, 1921

DEAR CHIEF:

I will try my best to give you some recollection of the Missions that visited America.... You will remember that I went down to Hampton Roads on the *Mayflower* to meet Joffre, Viviani and Chocheprat, and had an opportunity of talking with them all the way up the river, before they got to Washington or saw any other government people. My outstanding impression was that none of them had any real idea of what America was really going to do to help in the war. . . . When I told Viviani and Joffre that we expected to go into the military and naval operations on the largest possible scale they seemed impressed and intensely gratified. . . .

There is one episode in the visit of the British Mission which I think I have told you of verbally. . . . The first week we were in the war I had been studying a map of European waters, had measured the distances across the English Channel, across the North Sea from Scotland to Norway and across the Strait of Otranto at the mouth of the Adriatic. I had examined the depths of the waters in those places, and had come to the conclusion that some kind of a barrier, if it could be worked out on the technical side, offered the proper strategical solution of keeping German submarines out of the Atlantic and out of the Mediterranean. I talked to several officers in Operations at that time and also to several people in the Bureau of Ordnance and all of them turned it down or paid very little attention to it with the single exception of Commander Fullenwider who told me that he thought we ought to work on a new type of deep sea mine as a possible solution of the problem, and he agreed with me on the strategic wisdom of the suggestion.

Within two or three days of this two other men came to me with practically the same idea in mind. The first of them was Colonel E. Lester Jones of the Coast and Geodetic Survey. . . . Harris, of Yards and Docks, also brought up a plan. . . . About the first week in May as I remember it Admiral de Chair turned up with the Balfour Mission and I spent a long time going over the possibility of closing off the North Sea and the Adriatic with him. He did not enthuse over the subject, and I talked also with Mr. Balfour who pointed out the diplomatic effect of closing up the three-mile stretch of water along the North Coast. . . . I also talked to Chocheprat about it and he seemed not only highly favorable but very enthusiastic. Both de Chair and Chocheprat agreed to let me know what their Navy people thought as soon as they got back. I received a letter from de Chair saying he had taken it up with the Admiralty, but that they did not consider any plan of blocking the North Sea as being favorable. That was about the first part of June. Chocheprat, on the other hand, wrote that the French Ministry of Marine were highly favorable. . . .

If you will remember, Admiral Benson also showed little enthusiasm during June, July and August of 1917, and it was only after Fullenwider had worked out a new type of mine that Operations really got behind the project. Then followed a good many weeks of delay before the British Admiralty agreed in a very half-hearted way to proceed with the mine barrage, and it was only the knowledge that we would go ahead with it anyway that led to their final assent. . . .

Very sincerely,

FRANKLIN D. ROOSEVELT

[General J. J. C. Joffre had been supreme commander of the French armies. Vice Admiral Paul Chocheprat was the French naval representative in Washington in 1917. Commander S. P. Fullenwider was chief of the mine section of the Bureau of Ordnance. Admiral F. R. Harris was chief of the Bureau of Yards and Docks. Admiral Dudley S. de Chair accompanied Balfour to Washington in 1917 as British naval representative.]

NEW YORK, Oct. 5, 1921

DEAR CHIEF:

It was mighty good of you to take the time to write me that nice letter. [Daniels' letter is missing.] I particularly appreciate it as I know how hard it must be for you to get a minute to attend to personal correspondence. I learned through eight years' practical experience that the Secretary of the Navy is a fairly busy person, but Howe assures me that it was really nothing compared to being the Editor of a real live newspaper, and when you add to that the task of writing a book I don't really see where meals and sleep find a place in your daily schedule at all. I promised two years ago to write a book, and while I have no newspaper on my hands I have not yet found a chance to take it up, so I realize just what it meant to write me such a nice long letter.

I know you will enjoy your trip through the West, and lectures have great advantages over political speeches because you can really say exactly what is in your mind without the horrible fear that you may be stepping on somebody's tender toes.

I am sure you will be glad to learn that the doctors are most encouraging and express great pleasure at the speed I am making towards complete recovery, but it is rather tedious to a young man who is not fond of sitting still, and your surmise regarding the stern determination of my "missus" not to let me proceed too rapidly, is absolutely correct. In fact, I already suspect that she has entered into an alliance with the doctors to keep me in the idle class long after it is really necessary.

I hope you will be in New York sometime and will find a chance to drop in to see me. Mrs. Roosevelt joins me in kind regards to you and yours.

Always sincerely yours,
FRANKLIN D. ROOSEVELT

While on a holiday at Campobello Island early in August, 1921, Roosevelt suffered his attack of poliomyelitis. Daniels said that the first time he called on Roosevelt after the attack, Roosevelt, from his bed, "hauled off and gave me a blow that caused me nearly to lose my balance. He said: 'You thought you were coming to see an invalid, but I can knock you out in any bout.' It was that stuff—there is no other word for it—that enabled him to rise superior to any physical or other handicap." [1]

RALEIGH, Dec. 12, 1921

MY DEAR FRANKLIN:

I have just returned from a six weeks' lecture trip where I have been speaking nearly every night. I saw your cousin in Washington and that was the first word I had heard since I had been on this trip.

Our mutual friend, Henry Collins Brown, sent me a copy of the New York *World* telling of the visit your friends paid you at the hospital. I wish I could have joined that great company. I am hoping to get to New York in January and will run in and have an old time chat with you and I hope I will find you improving continually and steadily.

My wife joins me in love to Mrs. Roosevelt and your mother and all good wishes and the hope that we shall have the pleasure of welcoming you into our home when you can come South.

Sincerely yours,

JOSEPHUS DANIELS

[Henry Collins Brown was a prolific writer on the history and architecture of New York City.]

1. Daniels, *The Wilson Era, Years of Peace*, p. 131.

RALEIGH, Feb. 20, 1922

DEAR FRANKLIN:

It made us both very happy to see you and your people and to find how well you are getting on. I hope you are soon to be out and about and am sure the next time I am in New York I will find you as fit as of yore.

We are building a new house and I am wondering if we could get the artist who made "The Return of the Mayflower" for you to make a copy and what it would cost. Will you ascertain and let me know at your convenience. From time to time as you find naval pictures, of which duplicates are offered, will you put me in touch with the seller?

It is gratifying that the Foundation goes well. My wife has $25,000 in sight in this State.

With love from the whole D. family to all in your home and your mother.

Faithfully and affectionately

JOSEPHUS DANIELS

[The Foundation was the Warm Springs Foundation established by Roosevelt as an aid to sufferers from infantile paralysis.]

NEW YORK, February 24, 1922

DEAR CHIEF:

I am writing to Mr. Bernard F. Gribble in London to ask him whether he would care to undertake another "Return of the Mayflower" and also a copy of the other picture which I have not yet seen—the "Rodman's Squadron at the Surrender of the German Fleet." The only objection to the latter picture is the presence of Sims standing alongside of Rodman on the quarter-deck.

By the way, have you seen the N. Y. *American* of this morning, February 24th? They prove pretty conclusively that a campaign is under way, with the knowledge and approval of Sims, designed to make him an admiral, and I am sorry to say that my friend Davis appears to be mixed up with it.

When I think that during my two months abroad I saw more sea-service with the American Navy than Sims did in two years, it makes me anxious to apply to Congress for a life appointment as Lord High Admiral or at least something one grade better than what Sims is seeking. If Sims is made an Admiral what rank are they going to give to the Rear-Admirals who actually commanded ships?

As a matter of fact, taking it by and large, Sims did a mighty good job in London. In other words, did what we expected him to do as the principal Naval representative in Europe at that time, without the authority over Operations or policies which Pershing had in the Army.

I will certainly remember you if I come across any naval pictures. Do you want any relating to the early wars—such as the War of 1812, etc. The trouble with this war is that there are practically no engravings, lithographs or other prints. The only record is photographic, supplemented by a very small number of original paintings. While I was in Paris I tried to purchase the original drawing of the remarkable picture of the Marines in Belleau Wood which came out in *L'Illustration*, but the artist wanted about five thousand francs and I fled!

Do tell Mrs. Daniels how proud we are of the splendid record North Carolina is making for the Foundation.

It was perfectly fine to see you both the other day and I was so much encouraged by your visit that I have actually taken to crutches, and succeeded in crossing the room twice without a crash!

As ever yours,
FRANKLIN D. ROOSEVELT

[After the war, Admiral Sims voiced strong criticism of President Wilson and Secretary Daniels. He charged that the Navy's failure to send its full force of destroyers and anti-submarine craft to European waters "prolonged the war four months and occasioned the loss to the Allies of 2,500,000 tons of shipping, 500,000 lives, and $15,000,000,000." Daniels refused to order a court-martial for Sims because, he said, he and Wilson did not wish to make a martyr of him. Sims was a full Admiral during the war but reverted to permanent rank of Rear Admiral when he gave up his command in Europe.]

RALEIGH, May 8, 1924

MY DEAR FRIEND:

It affords me some satisfaction to know that I am not the only "squaw" man in the country. I was in Baltimore with my wife last week . . . and we were very much interested in the article in the New York *World*. I think the *World* showed good taste when it announced that you were taking the helm of the Smith campaign, they published the picture of your wife.

I have had that same experience on similar occasions and I have always wondered how the newspaper men knew so well who was at the head of the family. . . .

Sincerely your friend,

JOSEPHUS DANIELS

NEW YORK, May 26, 1924

DEAR CHIEF:

I loved your letter of May 8th. You are right about the squaws! Like you I have fought for years to keep my name on the front page and to relegate the wife's to the advertising section. My new plan, however, seems admirable—Hereafter for three years my name will not appear at all, but each fourth year (Presidential ones) I am to have *all* the limelight. Why don't you adopt this too? It will make it much easier to put that Democratic national ticket of Daniels and Roosevelt across in 1928 or 32. There is still, of course, a chance in this year of grace—if things come to the pass of keeping us all in New York until the 255th ballot on July 31st you and I can end the deadlock dramatically and effectively by putting your present candidate and mine into a room together armed with a complete Navy outfit ranging from bean soup to 16" guns with orders that only one man come out alive. Probably neither will come out alive and a grateful convention will give *us* the nomination by acclamation.

Do be sure to come right up and see us as soon as you drop anchor in New York. I understand your candidate has 850 delegates pledged to him—mine has 849—day and night shifts are now engaged in enlarging Madison Square Garden.

I do hope your wife is all right again—we all join in warm regards to you both.

As ever yours,
FRANKLIN D. ROOSEVELT

[Roosevelt was for Al Smith. Daniels was for William G. McAdoo. John W. Davis won the nomination, but not, of course, the election.]

RALEIGH, May 31, 1924

MY DEAR MR. ROOSEVELT:

I was very glad to receive your letter. My wife will be with me in New York and we are looking forward to see you and Mrs. Roosevelt and your mother.

I have received a letter today from a gentleman from New Jersey now living in Asheville, in which he says:

"As far as the probable choice of the highly intelligent population of New Jersey can be predicted, there is only one other man as well liked as Governor Smith, namely: Mr. Franklin D. Roosevelt. He is not running. He is young. The President should be young and strong, however."

So you see, you are likely to be the dark horse.

I am enclosing you a clipping that shows that our original ticket has some support in the La Follette camp.

My wife, who has been in the hospital, is much better and joins me in warm regards to all in your home.

Sincerely yours,
JOSEPHUS DANIELS

NEW YORK, June 18th, 1924

DEAR CHIEF:

Very many thanks for the *Life of Woodrow Wilson*. It looks delightful but I will not have a chance to read it until after I see you and the big work of the Convention is over.

Do let me know where Mrs. Daniels and you will be.

As ever,
FRANKLIN D. ROOSEVELT

[Daniels published his *Life of Woodrow Wilson* in 1924.]

In 1924 the Democrats nominated John W. Davis, a conservative, as their presidential candidate. Daniels and Roosevelt were extremely unhappy but supported Davis nevertheless. Because of the great dissatisfaction of many voters, who did not wish to vote for Davis or Calvin Coolidge, the Republican nominee, the Progressive Party was organized and nominated Senator Robert M. La Follette of Wisconsin as its presidential

candidate. An effort was made to persuade Daniels to accept
the Progressive Party's vice presidential nomination. Despite
his disapproval of Davis, however, Daniels believed that he
should "stick with the party." Coolidge won easily.

HYDE PARK, December 5, 1924

MY DEAR MR. DANIELS:

A number of acknowledged leaders of our Party have asked
my opinion as to what should be done to make the Democracy
a stronger and more militant organization nationally. In recent
years and in many States we have succeeded in electing Democratic governors. Yet these same States we fail to carry for our
presidential candidates. It is fair to reason that the Party organization is far weaker nationally than locally.

Before expressing my own views as to a remedy I want the
counsel and thought of representative Democrats throughout
the country. Therefore I am writing to every Delegate to the
recent National Convention, and I would sincerely appreciate
your views, expressed as fully and frankly as may be. What
you write me I will of course treat as confidential unless you
expressly give me permission to quote you.

I take it that we are all agreed on certain fundamental truths:

1. That the National Committee, or its executive machinery,
should function every day in every year and not merely in
presidential election years.

2. That the National Committee should be brought into far
closer touch with the State organizations.

3. That the executive machinery for year in and year out
work should be put on a continuing and business-like financial
basis.

4. That publicity for fundamental party policy and for the dissemination of current information should be greatly extended.

5. That party leaders from all sections should meet more frequently in order to exchange views and plan for united party action.

Something must be done, and done now to bring home to the voting population the true basis and sound reasons why the Democratic Party is entitled to national confidence as a governing party. There is room for but two parties. The Republican leadership has stood and still stands for conservatism, for the control of the social and economic structure of the nation by a small minority of hand-picked associates. The Democratic Party organization is made more difficult by the fact that it is made up in chief part by men and women who are unwilling to stand still but who often differ as to the methods and lines of progress. Yet we are unequivocally the party of progress and liberal thought. Only by uniting can we win.

It is not, I take it, a matter of personalities or candidates, but a matter of principles. If in the next three years we stop wasting time in booming or opposing this man or that for a nomination four years away, and devote ourselves instead to organizing for party principles, for the taking advantage of our opponents' errors and omissions, and for presenting our own logical and progressive program, we shall gain the confidence of the country; and find it far easier to choose a representative and successful ticket when the time comes.

I shall greatly appreciate it if you will write me.

Very sincerely yours,

FRANKLIN D. ROOSEVELT

RALEIGH, December 15, 1924

MY DEAR FRANKLIN:

I am in receipt of your letter and I am in entire accord with your point of view. What we need is a constructive chairman with such capacity as to take advantage of the mistakes of the Administration and to paramount the great principles of our party. The times are not very prosperous and there will be a reaction. Of course, if we have very prosperous times, the Republicans can carry the next Congress, but not otherwise. I agree with you that we shall not make any progress if we try to talk about candidates or organize in the interest of a new party.

I hope to be in New York in the early spring and will come to see you. I wish I could get away and go up to the dinner to Viscount Cecil, but I am unable to do so.

My wife sends her love to Mrs. Roosevelt.

Always sincerely your friend,

JOSEPHUS DANIELS

P.S. The election in New York demonstrates that our friend, Al Smith, is a wizard at getting votes.

[Lord Robert Cecil, the first Viscount Cecil of Chelwood, was President of the League of Nations Union. In 1924, he was a member of the Baldwin Cabinet, as chancellor of the duchy of Lancaster.

[In 1924 Alfred E. Smith won his third term as Governor of New York, defeating Theodore Roosevelt, Jr., the Republican candidate, by 1,627,111 votes to 1,518,552. Smith won his race although the Republicans won the presidential campaign with the election of Calvin Coolidge.]

RALEIGH, October 1, 1926

MY DEAR FRIEND:

I read your speech at the State Convention with great interest and pleasure and to quote the words of Louis Howe, "It was a masterpiece." I read through it pretty carefully, to see what you would have to say about the prohibition question and wondered how you would handle it. It seemed to me to call for all the diplomacy and wisdom of a Solomon to discuss it wisely without getting too wet. I think you took only a light bath and came out in fine shape. From that speech nobody would call you an immersionist like Al Smith; they would rather think you took yours by sprinkling or pouring. . . .

Sincerely yours,

JOSEPHUS DANIELS

[Daniels, of course, was a strict prohibitionist all his life. He and Roosevelt never agreed on this subject, but, although it was one of the burning issues of the day, it did not seriously affect the relationship of the two men as it often affected the relationships of other men at the time.]

WARM SPRINGS, GA., April 27th, 1927

DEAR CHIEF:

It is good to see your signature again. . . .

How are you and yours? I shall be here till May 15 and then in N. Y. or Hyde Park all summer. I do want to see you and talk about many things. Be sure to let me know if you come to N. Y. Down here we are accomplishing great results and will have 50 patients this summer—mostly infantile paralysis cases—I myself am getting on excellently—can walk with canes now—general health 100%—but even at that I'm not a candidate for any nomination in 1928, even though Hoke Smith and Clark Howell are booming me!

Faithfully,

FRANKLIN D. ROOSEVELT

[Hoke Smith was United States Senator from Georgia from 1911 to 1921. Clark Howell was publisher of the Atlanta *Constitution*.]

NEW YORK, June 23, 1927

DEAR CHIEF:

. . . I have just returned to New York and am trying to take stock of the situation. I don't have to tell you how much I appreciate what you said about me in your last letter [this letter is missing] but, frankly, I am very sure the situation prevents and will prevent even the suggestion of my name as a possible compromise between the existing warring factions. I do not think that we can *elect* any compromise choice, but on the other hand, I think we would stand an excellent chance of electing Governor Smith if we could nominate him. The chief point to be considered is that while a compromise choice of some perfectly worthy person would insure to us the electoral vote of the solid south and perhaps a few of the smaller western states, such a candidate could not possibly (if the election were tomorrow) carry a single one of the larger states of the east or middle west, and while probably doing better than John W. Davis, could not possibly get 266 votes in the electoral college. . . .

I assume, wrongly perhaps, that in the final analysis the southern states, with the possible exception of Tennessee and Kentucky, would as usual go Democratic. . . .

All of the above is perhaps nearly [merely?] practical politics. There is another side to it. I believe that Smith would make an unusually good President and would consolidate the party once more into a position of national strength.

It would make no difference with Smith personally if a compromise were named and he would undoubtedly throw his own personal hearty support to such a compromise. His adherents would refuse to listen to his plea and would vote the Republican ticket in large numbers, with the foolish idea that they were getting even with the Democratic party for an act of what they would call prejudice.

Strictly between ourselves, I am very doubtful whether any Democrat can win in 1928. It will depend somewhat on whether the present undoubted general prosperity of the country continues. You and I may recognize the serious hardship which the farmers in the south and west are laboring under, but the farmers in the south will vote the Democratic ticket anyway and I do not believe that the farmers of the west will vote the Democratic ticket in sufficient numbers even if they are starving.

Well, that is a very informal chatty letter to give you some of my thoughts. I do hope that you will come up to New York this summer and I am wondering whether you and Mrs. Daniels cannot come up and spend a Sunday with us all at Hyde Park. I expect to be here in town during the middle of each week and at Hyde Park from Friday to Mondays all summer except for the last week of July when I may have to take a hurried trip to Warm Springs, Ga., to attend the opening of my new golf course there under the auspices of the famous Bobby Jones. You and I must have a good heart to heart talk as soon as possible!

As ever yours,

FRANKLIN D. ROOSEVELT

[Roosevelt's doubts about the ability of the Democrats to win in 1928 were soundly based. But his belief that the farmers of the West would not vote the Democratic ticket "even if they are starving" was not borne out by the results of his own campaign in 1932. The South and the West voted heavily for Roosevelt. The same sections of the farming West that voted for Bryan in 1896 voted for F.D.R. in 1932.]

RALEIGH, July 19, 1927

MY DEAR FRANKLIN:

I have been away from home and that is my explanation for the delay in answering your letter.

This is the first time in my life that I have felt so perfectly at sea as to what we ought to do and what we can do. The liquor question is much more acute than it appears on the surface; the religious question, which ought not to exist but which does on both sides; and the hero-worship of Smith to which you refer; and the lack of any other leader with commanding support all combine to muddy the water so that it will take a keener eye than I possess to see to clear water.

There is nobody but McAdoo around whom the dry forces could unite and so many of his friends have advised him not to run that I think he is definitely out of it. At any rate, he is doing nothing; and when I saw him in Washington a few weeks ago, I gathered from his conversation that he had no intention of seeking the nomination. I believe that if he had been nominated in 1924, before the bitter feeling of Madison Square, he would have polled the labor vote and he would have won the party many of the dissatisfied farmers in the West, but I do not think he could have been elected, and I am quite sure Smith could not have been elected. Perhaps nobody could.

I think it is a thousand pities, looking back upon it, that we did not nominate either Smith or McAdoo so that we could have been freed of the issue, which is stronger than either of the men. It looks like the supporters of Smith—I do not mean Smith as a man—but the thousands of his supporters, feel that if he were not a Catholic he would be nominated, therefore, the large majority of them would be alienated by the nomination of any one else.

We have tried compromise candidates twice, first Cox and then Davis, with such results as I quite agree with you do not promise any good results in 1928. I have no idea that Governor Smith could be elected, but I say that with the consciousness that I am not well posted. There are a great many people who do not believe he could carry North Carolina. I am not certain about it. My own feeling is that he would carry it after a very hard fight, but it would tear us up in the Piedmont and Western parts of the State....

My wife sends her love to Mrs. Roosevelt.

Always with warm regards, I am

Faithfully yours,

JOSEPHUS DANIELS

[Smith did not carry North Carolina in 1928.]

RALEIGH, December 10, 1927

MY DEAR FRANKLIN:

When I was in your office I noticed some very beautiful prints of old ships. Could copies of some of them be obtained; and if so, from whom? Will you not put me in touch with such persons?

Always with my warm regards, I am,

Sincerely yours,

JOSEPHUS DANIELS

NEW YORK, December 13, 1927

DEAR CHIEF:

If you start in to collect prints of old ships, you might just as well sell the *News and Observer*, and with the proceeds you could make the beginnings of a collection! Years ago when I started to pick them up practically nobody else was in the field. For instance, those large colored prints of Clipper Ships which you saw in my office, I bought for $5.00 a piece. To-day, those same prints are bringing from $200 to $400 a piece.

Most of mine I have picked up in the auction rooms waiting for bargains, and very few of them have been bought since the great demand for them and a consequent rise in prices during the past ten years.

However, the next time you are in New York drop in to Max Williams, 805 Madison Avenue, or Robert Fridenberg, 22 W. 56th Street. Both of them carry a pretty good line of ship pictures and while their prices are high, they are not pirates.

The next time you come to New York, I do hope you will give me advance notice and come and dine with all of the family. My wife was very cross that I did not bring you home with me the other day. Also, there are a lot of matters, political and otherwise, which I did not get a chance to discuss with you.

With warm regards to you all,

Always faithfully yours,

FRANKLIN D. ROOSEVELT

P.S. A very wise old Republican leader from the middle West said to me today: "If you Democrats don't fall apart you *may* win in '28 and will surely win in '32." Keep up thy courage.

RALEIGH, December 17, 1927

MY DEAR FRANKLIN:

No wonder you thought I was entering upon a cruise that would require a Midas to finance because I did not make myself clear. What I intended to ask you was if there had not been copies made of some of the old prints. . . . I shall have to be content with the pictures which I have. The one that I prize most is a beautiful one you gave me of the old ship *North Carolina* which has a prominent place in our library. . . .

I am trying to follow your Quaker counsel 'Keep up thy courage.' I have never lost it yet and I am hopeful that the light will appear.

Always with my warm regards, I am

Sincerely yours,

JOSEPHUS DANIELS

RALEIGH, June 18, 1928

MY DEAR FRANKLIN:

. . . The attitude of the New York *World*, saying that Smith is "irretrievably a wet and as a wet he must run" and the talk of some of his supporters that there will be a wet plank, has greatly alarmed our people. If the Convention should nominate him on a wet plank he could not carry North Carolina, and I hope you will convey that information to the people who are writing the platform, because Smith, having a majority of the vote, could adopt a platform calling for a wet plank. If he should be nominated with such a plank it would be fatal in the South. His nomination would make North Carolina, in any event, a doubtful state; but with the hard work we would all do I think we could carry it for him with an enforcement pledge but any attempt to weaken the prohibition law or failure to pledge enforcement would make it impossible. The situation is more serious in North Carolina than the vote in the [State] Convention indicated. But, we will talk about all these matters when we get to Houston because I know that you and I, even if we differ about candidates, will wish to do the thing that will be wisest for the country and the party.

I sincerely wish that the situation was such that we could nominate you. I believe under the present conditions in the country you would have a better chance of election than any man we have. The Democratic Party would not only be defeated, but humiliated if the prohibition issue is paramounted. It seems to me that we have a great opportunity if we can make the big issue privilege and its twin brother, corruption. They always go together. We must get away from paramounting prohibition and we could only do this by enforcing the law.

My wife sends her love to Mrs. Roosevelt.

Always faithfully yours,

JOSEPHUS DANIELS

Daniels' counsel was politically sound, but the Smith forces won in the Houston Convention. F.D.R. put Smith's name before the Convention in a speech that won Roosevelt many friends. Daniels was unhappy but supported the party nominee.

On the prohibition issue and the religious issue the South was in opposition. Whether Smith would have had a chance if one of the issues could have been removed is doubtful. Together they made his defeat inevitable and overwhelming. But F.D.R. was elected Governor of New York while Smith lost the State to Herbert Hoover. As a gubernatorial candidate, Smith had won in Republican years. The fact that he could not carry the State in 1928 and the fact that F.D.R. did carry it hurt Smith deeply. He was never again "the Happy Warrior," a title Roosevelt had given him.

WARM SPRINGS, July 3, 1928

MY DEAR CHIEF:

I want to send you this line to congratulate you and thank you for the fine stand you have taken. Of course, you are dead right that the President can only recommend to Congress, that the Eighteenth Amendment is a part of the Constitution and that no old law can be modified or new law passed in such a way as to nullify the Constitution itself. I regard the platform as the strongest kind of indorsement of honest law enforcement—not only this law, but every other law.

The New York *World* makes me tired. Some day when I see you, I will tell you of my fight against Governor Ritchie and a few others who tried to upset all that had been accomplished in the preliminary work on the platform.

It was a joy to see you again and I only wish that you and I had had a chance to have a real old fashioned talk.

Do let me know if you come to New York this summer. Why don't you and Mrs. Daniels make a definite decision to spend a Sunday with Eleanor and me at Hyde Park? I get back next week and we shall be at Hyde Park every week end from then on.

As ever yours,

FRANKLIN D. ROOSEVELT

[Albert C. Ritchie was Governor of Maryland from 1920 to 1935.]

RALEIGH, July 6, 1928

DEAR FRANKLIN:

It is very good to get your love letter from Warm Springs, Georgia, and I assure you as the years go by our affectionate regard deepens.

While I could not vote for the nomination of Smith. . . . I was proud of the clear-cut, strong and able speech you made. A friend of mine here who was violently anti-Smith heard it over the radio and speaking of it, said to me: "It almost persuaded me." I think it fully persuaded him. . . .

Faithfully yours,
JOSEPHUS DANIELS

NEW YORK, July 20, 1928

DEAR CHIEF:

. . . I am still doing my best to line up the campaign issues on something other than this Wet and Dry question. Frankly, I am disturbed, but as you know, the campaign is very young yet and past history shows that the true issues are apt to come out during September, and the false issues be relegated to the background. I pray this may be so this year.

Frankly, I am more and more disgusted and bored with the thought that in this great nation, the principal issue may be drawn into what we do or do not put into our stomachs. Are there no great fundamentals of the science and practice of government left?

All of which is a mere preface to the real point of this letter: I hope and trust that the south, as a whole, will maintain its sense of proportion and that those who are now discouraged, will gradually come back during the next three months to full support of the old Party and of all its nominees.

Very sincerely yours,
FRANKLIN D. ROOSEVELT

New York, July 26, 1928

Dear Chief:

I am glad to see your fine and well received editorial of the 21st. I hope that, as the campaign progresses, three obvious facts will become more apparent in the south:

First, that no matter what Smith, as President, may recommend to Congress in regard to laws carrying out the Eighteenth Amendment the whole control of that situation rests with Congress itself.

Second, that Hoover, as President, will in all probability make just as much of a fiasco of prohibition enforcement as has been made by Coolidge, Mellon and the Republican administration during the past eight years. Surely even Bishop Cannon cannot be satisfied with the existing conditions.

Third, perhaps before November the voters will realize that there are several issues besides prohibition—and surely on these other issues there can be no question of how the south should decide as between Smith and Hoover.

Finally, there is one fact which makes my blood boil as a Protestant of a long line of wholly Protestant ancestry. These fool Methodist and Baptist ministers have been going around—a very large part of them—talking about what would happen if a Catholic were elected President and against the activities of the Catholic church in political matters. Now, these same gentlemen are taking a deliberate and active part in American politics not just as mere individuals, but as official representatives of their own Protestant churches. Somehow that does not appeal to me as being the kind of American fair play that we preach about.

Drop me a line from time to time as to how you think the situation is developing.

Always sincerely,

FRANKLIN D. ROOSEVELT

[Andrew W. Mellon was Secretary of the Treasury from 1921 to 1932. Bishop James Cannon of the Methodist Episcopal Church, South, was a fiery prohibition leader. In 1928, he was chairman of the Committee of Anti-Smith Democrats. Herbert Hoover was the Republican presidential nominee.]

NEW YORK, August 28, 1928

DEAR CHIEF:

I guess you and I are both all wet. I was not quite so dry as you were when we started for Albany, but you got wetter than I did. You see, we New Yorkers know well how to take precautions against moisture. I sat under an old navy tarpaulin and blessed you for the dry order.

I like your editorials and I hope you are sending them to the papers all over the south and to the dry sections of the west.

Word comes to me from Georgia that the opposition to Smith is eliminating itself by over-playing its hand. The more these vicious stories are circulated during the next two or three weeks, the greater will be the revulsion of feeling against them in November.

The next time you come to New York I insist on your bringing Mrs. D. with you. It will not do to have a repetition of the scandal of your last visit when you disappeared entirely for most one day and all of one night. It was all I could do to keep it out of the Metropolitan press.

As ever,

Yours,

FRANKLIN D. ROOSEVELT

[undated]

DEAR FRANKLIN:

Here is my article on Wilson and Prohibition. The exact words used by Wilson in his last utterance in Washington was:

"The Eighteenth Amendment should remain unchanged.

"The Volstead Act should remain unchanged."

I am standing now on the Houston platform and which-ever declaration I see, you got wringing wet at Albany. Franklin, I did not think it of you, but I dare say you are dry now.

Sincerely,
JOSEPHUS DANIELS

[This undated letter was apparently written from Raleigh during the 1928 campaign. In the 1920's, F.D.R. was neither wet nor dry, but he was a supporter of Smith, who was wet. In 1930 he came out for repeal of the 18th Amendment.]

RALEIGH, November 9, 1928

MY DEAR FRANKLIN:

I did not telegraph you because I have hardly adjusted myself to new conditions. I was so confident that Governor Smith would carry New York and adjacent states and the South that the result came as a great shock, and nothing was quite so great a shock as New York and North Carolina, which I felt were perfectly safe.

Two bright spots in the election this year, despite the "crack of matter or crash of worlds" that lighted up things were your election as Governor of New York and the elec-tion of Mr. Gardner as Governor of North Carolina. He is young and vigorous and of your type, so that with two such Governors in the two States we shall fight our way back. You have no idea how happy it made us all to see you come through in such great shape. It was a great tribute to you and a high honor and I wish for you the largest measure of success and usefulness. I hope before a great while to have a talk with you after the smoke clears away.

My wife joins in love to you and Mrs. Roosevelt.

Always faithfully yours,

JOSEPHUS DANIELS

[Herbert Hoover defeated Smith in the November election and split the solid South. Smith lost his own state of New York to Hoover, but F.D.R. was elected governor. North Carolina went for Hoover but elected as its governor, O. Max Gardner, a Democrat and friend of both Daniels and Roosevelt.]

WARM SPRINGS, GA., November 15, 1928

MY DEAR CHIEF:

I have your delightful letter while I am down here in Georgia for rest and treatment.

While I am delighted with the results in the State election in New York, where we saved most of the State ticket, and also to know that you saved your State ticket in North Carolina, the victories are clouded by the result in the Nation election, for, like yourself, I was confident that the Governor [Smith] would carry New York and enough of the other states to insure his election.

However, it is well worth remembering that the Governor has polled at least six million more votes than any previous Democratic candidate, and, as a matter of fact, the increase in the Democratic vote is far larger than that of our opponent. Certainly the party is by no means out of the running.

As I passed through the Old North State Saturday I was often reminded of you. I shall be here for some weeks yet, and as I have a cottage and a cook convenient, I wonder if you couldn't run down for a few days. It would be fine to have you. Please remember me to Mrs. Daniels.

Very sincerely yours,
FRANKLIN D. ROOSEVELT

RALEIGH, December 31, 1928

TELEGRAM TO ROOSEVELT

I have just read your inaugural address and send you my congratulations and felicitations in which my wife and sons join. With warm regards to you and your family and confidence that your administration will reflect credit upon you and redound to the good of your commonwealth.

JOSEPHUS DANIELS

Roosevelt was inaugurated Governor of New York on January 1, 1930. He opened his inaugural address with a warm tribute to Governor Smith, who was on the platform with him. Then he outlined a liberal program "to secure more of life's pleasures for the farmer; to guard the toilers in the factories and to insure them a fair wage and protection from the dangers of their trades; to compensate them by adequate insurance for injuries received while working for us; to open the doors of knowledge to their children more widely; to aid those who are crippled and ill; to pursue with strict justice, all evil persons who prey upon their fellow men; and at the same time, by intelligent and helpful sympathy, to lead wrongdoers into right paths."

ALBANY, January 3, 1929

DEAR CHIEF:

Thank you very much for your telegram of congratulations and good wishes. I wish so much that you all could have been here with us.

Very sincerely yours,
FRANKLIN D. ROOSEVELT

WARM SPRINGS, May 27, 1929

DEAR CHIEF:

I am enclosing a clipping from an up-state New York newspaper. Is there any way in which you can give me the facts in regard to Davidson County? I think I might be able to use them to advantage in my effort to get at the bottom of wasteful government in my state.

I had hoped to be able to arrange to stop off in Raleigh on my way North to see you all, but I have to fill an engagement here next Saturday evening and leave immediately to fill an engagement in New York on Monday.

My best to all of you, in which Eleanor joins.

As ever yours,
FRANKLIN D. ROOSEVELT

[Davidson County, N. C., had a county-manager plan of government that had been highly praised for its honesty and efficiency.]

RALEIGH, November 29, 1929

MY DEAR FRANKLIN:

Will you please be good enough to write me your recollection of a contract which was prepared and presented in the spring of 1919 while I was in Europe with reference to the General Electric Corporation of America? ...

Upon my return we talked over the contract and I recommended, with the approval of the President, that radio be entirely under the control of the Navy as a governmental monopoly....

With my warm regards,

Sincerely yours,

JOSEPHUS DANIELS

WARM SPRINGS, GEORGIA, Dec. 5, 1929

MY DEAR CHIEF:

Thanks for your note. I am down here for ten days but have to leave tomorrow rather suddenly to attend the funeral of Assemblyman [Maurice] Bloch, the Democratic Minority leader.

In regard to the radio corporation my general recollection is as follows: While you were in Europe a proposal was made by Mr. Owen Young and other representatives, chiefly of the General Electric Company, for the purchase of the navy owned stations and patents. As I recollect it the first proposition was to sell them to *a* Radio Corporation of America which was not to be clearly and definitely under American ownership. In other words, the Marconi company of England was to have a very large interest in it, if not half of, the control. Even before you got back I had told Mr. Young definitely that the Navy Department could not even consider the sale of any of its war acquired patents or stations to any company which was not wholly under American ownership.

Thereafter, on your return, we discussed the matter and

all agreed that we should ask Congress to retain complete control of radio throughout the United States as a government monopoly to be managed by the Navy in the beginning and perhaps later by some form of joint control in which the Department of Commerce and the Shipping Board could have a say. I recollect definitely that the President gave his approval to this plan and that you put it up to Congress, but that it was pigeon-holed up there, chiefly because there was so much to do in the way of demobilization, and because the sentiment that time was in favor of getting rid of as much government responsibility for every new thing as could be done.

It is my recollection that later on, either in the autumn of 1919 or in the spring of 1920, Mr. Young and his associates again came to Washington, this time with a plan for the organization of a radio corporation which would be wholly under American ownership and that, failing to obtain approval for the government monopoly, a reluctant consent was given to the transfer of the navy patents and stations to the radio corporation. . . .

Does this agree with your recollection? The one point I am absolutely certain about is that I personally and flatly turned down the first proposition of Owen Young because of the un-American ownership in the scheme. And I am equally certain that I was in hearty accord with the proposal for permanent government control until such time as it was clearly impossible to get it from Congress.

I have not had opportunity before this to tell you how very deeply appreciative I am for that wonderful day in Raleigh. Every minute of it was delightful and it was especially nice to see you and all the family again. I do hope that if you come to New York this winter for the A.P. meeting or any other event that you and Mrs. Daniels will run up to Albany and stay with us.

Always sincerely,
FRANKLIN D. ROOSEVELT

[Owen D. Young was president of the General Electric Corporation.]

ALBANY, N. Y., March 11, 1930

DEAR CHIEF:

That is a wonderfully clear editorial of yours. I am reminded of the remark which was made by a gentleman of New York about a year ago. He said "The New York *World*, in its instability, in its lack of proportion, did more to take votes away from Alfred E. Smith in his Gubernatorial and Presidental campaigns than any and all efforts of the Republican party combined."

The Lord preserve us from *some* of our friends.

As ever yours,
FRANKLIN D. ROOSEVELT

RALEIGH, March 13, 1930

MY DEAR FRANKLIN:

The last paragraph of your letter recalled a statement made during the Wilson administration which correctly portrays the attitude of our esteemed contemporary.

He said: "Frank Cobb's editorials, backing the administration, are the best things that appear in any American journal. But, just about the time the country begins to say that the *World* is supporting the administration and is a Democratic journal, in order to show its independence, it will come out and administer a severe spanking upon some great policy of the administration, just to show that it is independent. It does not make any difference that the measure denounced is the best Wilson ever proposed and that it is along the line of many commended in the *World*, the time has come for the spanking and the *World* administers it with a slipper. And, having done this, and thereby made impotent all the good service it has rendered, it comes back to the support of the administration, with a wink to its readers, saying, 'Look at us! We spank our own just to show that we can do it.' "

Sincerely yours,

JOSEPHUS DANIELS

Frank Cobb was the distinguished editor of the New York *World*, a leading Democratic organ which frequently annoyed Daniels and Roosevelt because of its independence. Daniels was always a party man, although his newspaper was often independent on major party issues. Nevertheless, Daniels was a partisan and many of his friends and supporters thought his paper could have rendered a greater service if he had been less partisan and if he had not played a direct role in Democratic politics. Daniels was advised by some of his friends not to join Wilson's Cabinet because such an act would necessarily mean that his paper would have to be less independent. Politicians are seldom patient with public criticisms, especially from friends and supporters. They look upon such criticism as an expression of disloyalty.

ALBANY, November 12, 1930

DEAR CHIEF:

It was particularly nice to get your telegram election night. Wasn't it a perfectly splendid victory throughout the country? I am especially heartened by the up-state vote here in New York, and I feel that we have a real organization—something to work with and something to give confidence to all of our workers.

I leave for Warm Springs next Monday. I am going to have three weeks of real rest and recreation I hope.

Eleanor and I both wish we could see you. Is there any possibility in the near future?

My best wishes to you and Mrs. Daniels in which Eleanor joins me.

Always sincerely,
FRANKLIN D. ROOSEVELT

Roosevelt was re-elected Governor of New York and the Democrats made notable gains throughout the country. The Republicans shortly afterward lost control of the House of Representatives. As the depression deepened, the party in power became increasingly unpopular.

RALEIGH, June 17, 1931

MY DEAR FRANKLIN:

I have been hoping that something would call me up to New York so that I could have a chat with you. First of all, I wish to send you and your mother my own and my wife's sincere regards and tell you of our great happiness to know that she is well again. You know in what high esteem we hold her and we were greatly distressed when we heard that she was ill in France.

All of us rejoiced here when you turned the tide at Washington and prevented the endorsement of Raskob's program. The situation in North Carolina is not yet fully shaped and we have of course some more or less factions in the party, but I want you to know that you have very many friends here who are hopeful of seeing you in the White House. I had a very long talk with the Governor this morning and he wished me to convey to you his feeling of friendship and admiration. If we can go to the country on the issues which Hoover has given us with your ringing declaration about the Hawley-Smoot bankrupt tariff and your record on the power issue and your splendid administration as Governor of New York, we can certainly win. Here in North Carolina, as in most of the South, the people are troubled about the prohibition question, as you know. The Governor feels, and so do I, if it should be in the forefront it might prove the lion in the path. We must respect the consciences of men who are opposed to prohibition and those who are in favor of it and seek a united party upon the vital issues, but I will talk to you about that sometime in the future.

In the meantime, I wish you to know that I am seeking to find the best way to promote our success in 1932 and, of course, with esteem for you and happiness that you have made such a great record as Governor of New York.

My wife sends her love to Mrs. Roosevelt.

Faithfully yours,
JOSEPHUS DANIELS

[John J. Raskob and Jouett Shouse, in alliance with Al Smith, were planning, at a meeting in March of the Democratic National Committee, to adopt a policy statement emphasizing the need for Prohibition repeal. F.D.R., who was now actively taking the lead in preparation for his campaign to win the presidential nomination in 1932, did not want to see the policy statement adopted. It would have caused a party row and increased the prestige of the Smith forces. Roosevelt wrote to a number of Committee members, and to Smith and Shouse, opposing the statement. It was never formally presented to the Committee, a fact duly noted and credited as a victory for the Roosevelt forces. James A. Farley was active for Roosevelt as were a large number of Democrats from the South and West. The Governor of North Carolina was O. Max Gardner.]

ALBANY, June 29, 1931

DEAR CHIEF:

I want to see you very much as I feel the need of all the good advice that I can get, particularly of those who have had long political experience and who I feel sure are my tried and trusted friends. I hope you can arrange to see me before very long. I am speaking in Charlottesville, Va., on Monday, July sixth, and shall arrive there late Sunday afternoon. I am wondering if it would be possible, in case the trip to New York is out of the question, for you to run up to Charlottesville and see me either Sunday night or sometime Monday....

Very sincerely yours,
FRANKLIN D. ROOSEVELT

RALEIGH, July 8, 1931

MY DEAR FRANKLIN:

It was a great delight to see you at Charlottesville and to see you looking so well and in such fine spirit.

Your speech was everything it should have been....

Please remember me with regards to Mrs. Roosevelt and all your family,

Faithfully yours,
JOSEPHUS DANIELS

[On July 6, Roosevelt spoke at the University of Virginia on the excessive costs and taxes in local government. "I am quite convinced," he said, "that the excessive cost of local government can most effectively be reduced by simplifying the local governmental organization and structure and by reallocating the responsibility for performing various services, according to a logical analysis rather than by accident or tradition." One trouble, he said, is that "we hate the details of government." People would rather talk about Russia's five-year plan or Mussolini's system than "whether a town supervisor is good for anything or . . . what a village health officer does to earn his pay."]

ALBANY, August 1, 1931

DEAR CHIEF:

At least I got one excellent result out of my Virginia trip—four days of constant exercise in a temperature above ninety degrees removed ten pounds from the particular spot where I wished most to lose it!

I was most interested to see the fine work that is being accomplished at Monticello and they tell me the visitors there are constantly increasing in number. Perhaps if we come into control in 1933, we can take some definite steps to make Monticello much more truly a national shrine than it is today. There are all sorts of possibilities there which I wish you would be turning over in your mind. Now that Virginia is getting excellent highways, there is no reason why a million people a year should not go there instead of fifty thousand. . . .

I haven't heard yet from Harry Byrd as to when he is to see Raskob. I gather for your ears alone that Raskob still hopes, at the meeting of the National Committee this fall, to force through some kind of resolution on various matters of policy. I am to see Shouse shortly but Raskob is apparently so angry with me that he does not even want to discuss matters. I do not particularly care but I do want to avoid a row this November or December. Our friends in Washington, such as Cordell Hull, are keeping close track of things.

I do not need to tell you what a real delight it was to see you at Charlottesville and it was a delight to find you in such fine form. Be sure to let me know the next time you come north, there will be many things to talk over. I still feel that this winter we shall face far more serious economic conditions. The Hoover administration apparently has no plans or program either national or international. They jumped into this German moratorium business on twenty-four hour notice and without previous study just because they were told by the New York Bankers that if Germany went into bankruptcy, the Stock Exchange in New York would close and most of our biggest banks would be seriously embarrassed! I think there is no question of the authenticity of this.

Now I am off on fairly continuous inspection trips through the State until I go to Warm Springs for three weeks holiday the end of September.

As ever yours,
FRANKLIN D. ROOSEVELT

P. S. Tell Mrs. Daniels that you and I have a deep secret from her relating to your conduct at the Fairlington Club but that neither you nor I will ever tell her.

[Harry F. Byrd was at this time vice chairman of the Democratic National Committee. He supported Roosevelt as against Raskob. Cordell Hull was Senator from Tennessee.]

RALEIGH, January 2, 1932

MY DEAR FRANKLIN:

I was very sorry not to have been able to come to Hyde Park.

I stopped by Washington for a day and I found the sentiment there all that you could desire. It is quite certain that Mr. Raskob can put through no platform and that the leaders of the party are not willing to jeopardize the victory that seems now in sight by attempting to write a platform by an unauthorized body. Your action last year in throwing the weight of New York State against the Raskob policy is everywhere appreciated and has won you innumerable friends.

Recent events prove the wisdom of your course in withholding discussion on national questions until after the National Convention is called. Hoover has no program except some poultices of doubtful value and there is no enthusiasm for him or in his party. All the friends that I saw feel that you will be nominated.

My wife and all the family join in regards and New Year greetings to you and yours.

Faithfully yours,
JOSEPHUS DANIELS

ALBANY, January 22, 1932

DEAR CHIEF:

It is good to get Frank's letter and to know that you are on your way home again. I am too sorry about the accident— it must have been most painful and I do hope that the arm is knitting quickly and that you will soon have the full use of it again. There is no question that editors should return to horse and buggy. Did you read that Frank Gannett was smashed up in South Carolina at the same time?

Do be sure to let me know if there is any chance of your coming to New York this winter. I do want to see you. As you know, my Legislature is at it again, but it looks now as if they will go along with almost all of my recommendations and adjourn by the middle of March.

My best to all in which Eleanor joins.

As ever yours,

FRANKLIN D. ROOSEVELT

[Frank Daniels, now general manager of the Raleigh *News and Observer*, was one of the four Daniels boys. Daniels had an auto accident in Atlanta. Frank E. Gannett was publisher of a chain of New York State newspapers.]

RALEIGH, February 5, 1932

MY DEAR FRANKLIN:

I am glad to say that I am back at home again. The accident was more serious than was indicated and the surgeons will not let me leave my home until the cast is taken off my arm, which will be two weeks from today. My left leg is pretty badly damaged but is improving and I am now able to walk from room to room. My head, which was bunged up, is healing nicely. You have probably had occasion before to suspect that I had a hard head but now that it has busted the top out of a Lincoln car you will know it....

My wife joins me in love to you and Mrs. Roosevelt.

Sincerely yours,

JOSEPHUS DANIELS

ALBANY, March 7, 1932

DEAR CHIEF:

Thank you ever so much for your nice letter. I am delighted that you are coming along so well and I do hope that I shall see you on my way to Warm Springs, if not sooner. Don't you think it would be a grand idea for you to come to Warm Springs for a while?

Eleanor joins me in love to you both.

Always sincerely,

FRANKLIN D. ROOSEVELT

RALEIGH, March 9, 1932

DEAR FRANKLIN:

I am very glad to receive your letter. It came this morning at the same time as the news from New Hampshire which is most gratifying. I hope it will teach the Raskob people a lesson and show them that the Democratic party is not going to repeat the blunders of 1928.

My wife sends her love to Mrs. Roosevelt. I wish very much I could go to Warm Springs but I have been in the hospital and at home for eight weeks now and while I cannot get to my office, I do some work at home though I am only half a man, but I hope before long to be able to get out. Let me know when you pass through on your way to Atlanta. I wish you could stop over.

With affectionate regards,

Faithfully yours,

JOSEPHUS DANIELS

[Roosevelt openly declared his candidacy for the Democratic nomination for President on January 22, 1932, by authorizing the Democratic State Committee in North Dakota to enter his name in the preferential primary. His victories during the following months were impressive. He won a sweeping victory over Al Smith in the New Hampshire primary, and in Iowa and Georgia, among others.]

RALEIGH, March 30, 1932

MY DEAR FRANKLIN:

Congratulations upon the result in Iowa, New Hampshire and Georgia! The American people like a man to be a good sportsman and they have been disappointed in Governor Smith's lack of that quality. I think you are pursuing the right course with reference to the matter. I have not had much to say about it and have been rather careful of what I did say, because the country knows of our friendship and might attribute it to you in some sense if I were to express my feeling, and, as a matter of fact, it would require asbestos paper to print what I think about Smith in the matter....

Faithfully yours,

JOSEPHUS DANIELS

RALEIGH, April 9, 1932

MY DEAR FRANKLIN:

You hit the bullseye in your radio speech....

We cannot win by letting the folks think the Republican party is 51% bad and we are only 49% bad. Some of our folks in Washington have thought if we acted not quite as subservient to the big interests as the Republicans we could win. You have shown them that we must have a definite policy and that prosperity cannot be invoked by incantations and lending money to people who do not use it to start the wheels of industry.

Faithfully yours,

JOSEPHUS DANIELS

[On April 7, F.D.R. delivered his "forgotten man" speech on a radio program sponsored by the Democratic National Committee. "These unhappy times," he said, "call for the building of plans that rest upon the forgotten, the unorganized but the indispensable units of economic power, for plans ... that put their faith once more in the forgotten man at the bottom of the economic pyramid."]

ALBANY, April 12, 1932

DEAR CHIEF:

That is a grand editorial on my radio speech. That I stepped on a good many toes is evident from the howl from the New York *Times* and other leading papers, which represent the school of thought which you and I have so often come into conflict with. . . .

I hope the arm is coming on well.

As ever,

FRANKLIN D. ROOSEVELT

RALEIGH, May 4, 1932

MY DEAR FRANKLIN:

. . . I had a talk yesterday with Governor Gardner, Governor McLean, Senator Bailey and others and we all think there is no doubt that North Carolina will send an instructed delegation for you to Chicago. So far there has been very little opposition . . .

I do not believe it is going to be possible to prevent your nomination. Of course Smith's policy is endangering our success in November, but I believe the people are so determined upon a change that you will be certain to be elected.

My wife sends love to Mrs. Roosevelt.

Faithfully yours,

JOSEPHUS DANIELS

[Angus W. McLean was Governor of North Carolina from 1925 to 1928. Josiah W. Bailey was Senator from North Carolina from 1931 to 1946.]

In a letter to Daniels from Warm Springs the next day, F.D.R. said that if the California and Texas delegations could be won over (California and Texas were for John N. Garner, Speaker of the House of Representatives) that "would cinch the matter" of his nomination. Roosevelt was exactly right. He was to go into the Convention with a clear majority. But he needed, and finally got, California and Texas to obtain the two-thirds vote necessary for the nomination.

RALEIGH, May 12, 1932

MY DEAR FRANKLIN:

I am enclosing an editorial that appeared in today's *News and Observer*. I hope you will like it.

Faithfully yours,

JOSEPHUS DANIELS

[In an editorial entitled "Why Roosevelt Is Sweeping On to the Nomination," Daniels said that F.D.R. was leading in the fight for the nomination because "the bulk of the people believe he will be adamant to Privilege and because the people have seen the selfish aims of certain elements opposing his candidacy."]

WARM SPRINGS, GEORGIA, May 14, 1932

DEAR CHIEF:

That is a grand editorial and you are right in hammering at the fact that the real opposition comes directly from the sources of special privilege. You and I went through the same big contest in 1912. We can only elect a Democrat who declines to have a halter round his neck and who appeals to the liberal soul of the country.

Confidentially, I understand that the Smith-Shouse-Raskob crowd really want Young, but that the latter declines to run and that they will turn with a deep sigh to Newton Baker. I don't need to tell you how much I admire and respect Newton and what a wonderful asset he can be to the Party during the next four years if we win. The trouble is that he labors under very definite political handicaps. Because of, or rather in spite of, his perfectly legitimate law practice he is labeled by many progressives as the attorney for J. P. Morgan and the Van Schweringens; he is opposed by Labor; he would be opposed by the German-Americans; and also by the bulk of the Irish because of his consistent League of Nations attitude up to this year. As they say, "them are the sad facts"! All of this seems a pity because New would make a better President than I would!

I think things are going all right and I honestly believe I shall have over six hundred votes when the first ballot is taken.

My best to you all.

As ever yours,

F.D.R.

[Owen D. Young was frequently mentioned as a Democratic presidential possibility. Newton D. Baker had been Secretary of War during World War I.]

Roosevelt's prediction that he would receive "over six hundred votes" on the first ballot was a good one. When the Convention took its first ballot at Chicago in June, F.D.R. received 666½ votes, 103½ short of the two-thirds vote then required for nomination. He gained slightly on the second and third ballots. Then came the shift to Roosevelt by Texas and California and his nomination on the fourth ballot.

ALBANY, June 16, 1932

TELEGRAM TO DANIELS

Perfectly delighted with good old North Carolina's action. My thanks with lots of love to you all.

FRANKLIN D. ROOSEVELT

RALEIGH, June 17, 1932

MY DEAR FRANKLIN:

As I telegraphed you yesterday, the State Convention practically unanimously instructed for you for President. We have a very good delegation, including Governor Gardner, ex-Governor McLean, Senator Bailey and others, and I am on as one of the delegates-at-large....

My wife joins in love to you and Mrs. Roosevelt.

Sincerely yours,

JOSEPHUS DANIELS

RALEIGH, June 18, 1932

MY DEAR FRANKLIN:

I take it that you are looking after the matter, but I am writing to suggest that if you have not already selected him that the best man for Chairman of the Platform Committee is Cordell Hull of Tennessee. He is sound to the core.

Faithfully yours,

JOSEPHUS DANIELS

In early 1932, Cordell Hull and other supporters of the Roosevelt candidacy prepared a draft platform for possible consideration by the party Convention. They discussed it on several occasions with Roosevelt. The draft was later adopted in large part by the Committee on Platform and Resolutions. Before the Convention met, Roosevelt told Hull he wanted him to be Chairman of the Platform Committee. "I thanked him but said that, while this was a high honor, I could be of more service by being footloose and remaining on the floor, where I could defend all provisions of the platform draft against attack," Hull wrote.[2]

ALBANY, July 26, 1932

DEAR CHIEF:

Every once in a while I recall stories of episodes in our Navy days, but it is awfully hard to think them up on the spur of the moment.

I remember very well, for instance, your sending me on the Mayflower to Hampton Roads with Mr. Bryan and Elihu Root to meet Senhor Lauro Muller, the Foreign Secretary of Brazil, and how I spent one horrible evening translating Doctor Muller's French and German with great difficulty to Mr. Bryan and Senator Root.

Eleanor and I did escort the Marshalls to the official opening of the San Francisco Exposition. I shall always remember the V.P. going on board Admiral Howard's flagship and getting so flustered as he went over the side that he shook hands with the side boys—but it would not do to print that story.

You will remember that under your direction I got Eliot

2. *The Memoirs of Cordell Hull* (New York, The Macmillan Company, 1948), I, 151.

Brown to build the Pelham Bay base at the outbreak of the war, and also the big base in the park in Brooklyn.

I have lots of material and lots of photographs, including my report to you when I got back from Europe the first time. The trouble is that all of these documents are in boxes in the cellar at Hyde Park and I cannot possibly get them out.

I am wondering if one of our friends in the Department—possibly F. S. Curtis—could not try to dip out some really interesting material from some of the Navy files.

I am sending a line to our old friend Doctor Martin as you suggest.

That cruise with the boys was a real rest and now the preliminary organization work seems to be going well. It is fine to know that you are going to the Legion meeting in Portland, Oregon, and also that you can make some speeches on the way back. Don't forget what you did for Puget Sound, for Mare Island, for San Pedro Harbor and San Diego. The Coast was never on the map from the Navy point of view until you put it there.

Everything seems to be going well. I probably cannot leave this State for another month because the Walker case will last that long.

Love to all of you.

As ever yours,

F.D.R.

[Daniels had been asked to write some magazine articles about Roosevelt, one of which appeared in the *Saturday Evening Post*, and he asked F.D.R. for help. He also suggested that the candidate write to Dr. Franklin H. Martin, director general of the American College of Surgeons, because of his influence with surgeons throughout the country. Thomas R.

Marshall was Vice President during Wilson's two terms. The "case" against Mayor James J. Walker of New York was brought by Judge Samuel Seabury and resulted in the resignation of Walker. Rear Admiral Thomas Benton Howard was Commander in Chief of the Pacific Fleet in 1914 and 1915.]

ALBANY, August 23, 1932

DEAR CHIEF:

I agree with you about the Special Session of the Congress and that we shall probably require it next April. It is my thought that I will hold such an announcement until early in October.

I hope you are getting a fine rest at the lake and I hope too that you liked my Columbus speech. Things in Ohio seem to be going well.

As ever yours,
FRANKLIN D. ROOSEVELT

[Roosevelt lashed out at the failures of the Hoover Administration in a speech on August 20 at Columbus, Ohio. The Administration, he said, "misunderstood the forces which were involved in the economic life of the country" and "encouraged a vast speculative boom." Finally, "it delayed relief; it forgot reform."]

ALBANY, September 12, 1932

DEAR CHIEF:

I am dictating this just before leaving for the big trip to the Coast, and I am glad that I had that 1920 experience, otherwise I should be worried by the prospect....

Love from us to you all.

As ever yours,
F.D.R.

Roosevelt began his major presidential campaign trip on September 12. He made important speeches in Topeka, Salt Lake City, Seattle, Portland, San Francisco, Sioux City and Detroit before returning to Albany in early October. Later he campaigned in the Mid-West and along the Atlantic seaboard as far south as Baltimore.

RALEIGH, September 26, 1932

MY DEAR FRANKLIN:

It was a great disappointment to me that I could not meet you while we were both in the West. In Oregon and California I was ahead of you about a week or ten days and in Utah and Nebraska I was ten days behind you. I spoke in Oregon, California, Nevada, Utah, Nebraska and Iowa and those states are much stronger for you now than they were for Wilson at the same time in 1916. I do not believe they can be taken away between now and election. . . .

Sincerely yours,
JOSEPHUS DANIELS

ELKHART, INDIANA, November 5, 1932

DEAR FRANKLIN:

This is the last time I will write you a letter beginning "Dear Franklin" though the change in title will not alter my affectionate greeting. After Tuesday, my letters will commence with "Dear Chief" and after the Fourth of March "Dear Mr. President."

From the day of my address to the Convention of the American Legion I have been almost constantly on the stump, covering states from Oregon and California to North Carolina, spending more time in California, Ohio and Indiana than in any other states. You may remember that I covered the same territory in 1916 and told you before the election that Wilson would carry most of those states. The sentiment this year from every indication and expression is many times stronger for you than it was for Wilson in 1916. I will be the worst fooled man alive if you do not carry nearly all of them. . . .

I congratulate you upon your magnificent and vote-winning campaign. I have followed it with admiration and pride. You have ended the campaign with millions of friends whose faith and esteem must give you gratitude and nerve you for the great tasks that lie before you. . . .

> Faithfully and affectionately,
> Your sincere friend,
> JOSEPHUS DANIELS

On November 8, 1932, Roosevelt won a sweeping victory. President Hoover carried only six states. Roosevelt carried forty-two and had a popular plurality of seven million votes.

RALEIGH, November 9, 1932

MY DEAR CHIEF:

You see I am giving you your new and proper appellation. There was a time when you used to address me in this fashion, but times change and positions change with them.

I am very happy to have been associated with one who through the years has grown to the place where he has harvested the affection and confidence of the great bulk of the American people. I was happy to see the words you employed with reference to this expression of the people and I have made some reference to it in an editorial in today's *News and Observer* and am enclosing a copy.

Nowhere in America outside the Roosevelt family is there more genuine happiness and satisfaction over the great victory than in our home. As I telegraphed you, this is personal and due to our affection, but it is also based upon confidence that you will meet the high expectations of your countrymen.

I do not need to tell you that I shall be jealous for the largest measure of success which you will achieve and that whenever you wish my counsel and advice and assistance, if they have any value, I hope you know you will only need to command me.

Always faithfully yours,
JOSEPHUS DANIELS

RALEIGH, November 10, 1932

MY DEAR FRANKLIN:

I am enclosing copy of a syndicate letter that I write every week and have marked a portion that I thought might interest you.

I am ambitious that your administration shall be followed by a strengthening of the Democratic party so that it will not henceforth be dependent upon the Southern States and three or four pivotal States, but that it shall be, as in the early days of the Republic, the dominant party in all parts of the country.

I hope sincerely to see you the leader who will so administer the affairs of the country and lead the party as to give us another regime such as inaugurated by Jefferson and carried on under Madison and Monroe, and, after a brief four years [of] John Quincy Adams, under Andrew Jackson. You say that is a very great ambition. So it is. But nothing less, I am sure, animates you. It can be done only by following your suggestion on the day after election that this was a victory of more than party and we shall be able to make the Democratic victory permanent only by serving the whole people in line with the platform and your campaign declarations.

Sincerely yours,

JOSEPHUS DANIELS

[In this letter of November 10, Daniels apparently forgot his promise to address the President-elect as "Dear Chief." The next letter from Roosevelt was in reply to Daniels' letter of November 9.]

ALBANY, NOV. 17, 1932

MY DEAR CHIEF:

That title still stands! and I am still Franklin to you.

I am sure you know how happy your letter makes me and also the fact that our friendship is so close. I am always grateful for your advice even though I do not always write to tell you so. I know that you take this for granted.

I am getting away to Warm Springs next week, but as you know must stop off at Washington to see the President.

My love to all your family in which my family joins me.

As ever yours,

FRANKLIN D. ROOSEVELT

[During his years in the White House only a very few people outside his immediate family addressed Roosevelt by his first name. Daniels was one of the few, and he was one of the very few who called Roosevelt by his first name with Roosevelt's blessing. There were some who called the President by his first name without his consent or approval, and F.D.R. did not like it.]

ALBANY, November 28, 1932

DEAR CHIEF:

It is always pleasant to find a letter from you in my mail and the one which expresses your ambition for the future is particularly welcome and significant.

You may be sure that I recognize both the great opportunities and the grave responsibilities which lie ahead of us all. It is good to know that I may count on you for the honest criticism and wise counsel which I associate with your name....

See you soon. Affectionate regards to you all.

Yours very sincerely,

FRANKLIN D. ROOSEVELT

[This letter, in reply to Daniels' letter of November 10, was almost certainly not written by Roosevelt himself but by a secretary. It is generally easy to spot a letter written for F.D.R.'s signature by a secretary. They are much more formal and full of long and stiff words seldom used by Roosevelt.]

RALEIGH, December 14, 1932

MY DEAR FRANKLIN:

From more than one source worthy of consideration I have heard the suggestion that it might be very wise if you would ask all the newly elected Governors to meet you for a conference on the subject of taxation and public expense....

You have doubtless thought about this but I venture to pass on to you what has come to me from several sources. If there is any good in it, you will adopt it.

Do not take time to answer. I know something of the stress you are under.

All the Daniels family send love to the Roosevelts.

Faithfully yours,

JOSEPHUS DANIELS

ALBANY, December 16, 1932

DEAR CHIEF:

I am already at work on exactly the suggestion you have made. It fits in with my campaign speech. The question is as to whether I should get the new Governors together before the 4th of March or immediately thereafter. One of the suggestions made relates to sales taxes which are now levied both by the Federal government and certain State governments. Where the State tax is very high there is a good deal of evasion—bootlegging of gasoline, etc. The suggestion is that in this case the Federal government should agree with the States to collect say 5¢ a package on cigarettes, the Federal government would increase this to 8¢ and return 1¢ to the States. I wish you would give me your slant on this. The danger is that it might result in all manner of future trouble and in too great an extension of the Federal taxing power.

As ever yours,

FRANKLIN D. ROOSEVELT

NEW YORK, January 5, 1933

DEAR CHIEF:

I liked what you said in Philadelphia, and wish I could have seen the whole speech.

I am working on the possibility of conferring with the Governors on March 6th—it depends on how far we get with this session of Congress and how far I shall be ready to talk along definite lines. I will know more about things after tonight. It looks like an extra session of Congress, but between ourselves I do not want to start it until I have time to turn around and survey things for several weeks.

As ever yours,

F.D.R.

NEW YORK, January 18, 1933

DEAR CHIEF:

... You are right about Roper. He will be of immense service, but I don't yet know just where.

As ever yours,

F.D.R.

[The reference to Roper in Daniels' letters is missing, but it is clear that Daniels had made a favorable reference to him. Daniel C. Roper, a South Carolinian, was slated to be Secretary of Commerce. In the next letter, undated but apparently written about the end of January, 1933, Daniels refers to the fact that some North Carolina leaders had endorsed him to receive the highest post to go to a North Carolinian.]

RALEIGH [January, 1933]

DEAR FRANKLIN:

I have been informed that some time ago, without my knowledge, the Chief Justice of the Supreme Court [Walter P. Stacy] and other leaders in this State wrote you expressing the hope that you would invite me to official connection with your administration. Just before his term as Governor expired, Governor Gardner, our National Committeeman, told me that, if it would not be embarrassing to me, he intended to see or write you and say that the Democracy of the State of North Carolina desired you to know that whatever position should come to North Carolina they desired you to give me first consideration. I am informed that Mrs. Jerman, our National Committeewoman, both our Senators and Hon. E. W. Pou, Dean of our Delegation in Congress, have written to the same effect. Mr. Pou, who is chairman of the Committee on Rules, writes me he called to see you when you were in Washington. I enclose you a copy of Mr. Pou's letter.

I told these leaders of the North Carolina Democracy that many friends in all parts of the country had written volunteering to write you suggesting my participation in the big work of your administration, but I had written that you knew me better than anybody else, and I did not wish them to write. Governor Gardner said to me: "Of course we would not presume to commend you to Governor Roosevelt. All we wish to do is to assure him of our desire that whatever honor is coming to North Carolina in his administration, the State wishes the highest to go to you." I consented because it has always been my belief that while no President should abdicate his right to fill presidential offices, it was the part of wisdom not to name a man from any state to a particular position (of course there are exceptions) unless it was agreeable to the delegation in Congress and the leaders of the party in his State. You know that one reason why we were able to carry the Navy Programs through so well from 1913 to 1920 was because we kept in close touch with Congressional leaders charged with naval appropriations.

You know of my deep and sincere interest in the success of your administration and my readiness to give such aid or support in any way as you may feel I can render.

With congratulations upon your birthday, and wishing you many more in health and happiness and with affectionate regards to you and Mrs. Roosevelt, I am

Faithfully yours,

JOSEPHUS DANIELS

[Mrs. Palmer Jerman was Democratic National Committeewoman from North Carolina from 1928 to 1934.]

The only reply to Daniels' letter was a form acknowledg-
ment from Louis M. Howe. But late in February, Daniels
saw Roosevelt in New York and had a long talk about the
problems of the new administration. Roosevelt asked Daniels
to go to Washington with him to make a study of transporta-
tion problems and to become Chairman of the Shipping Board.

"I agreed to go to Washington and make an independent
study, first of the Shipping Board, and then tell him what
I thought should be done with it before accepting or declin-
ing the chairmanship," Daniels recalled later. "He said he had
been so engrossed with other matters that he had deferred
specific plans and would like my suggestions and my administration of them. Also, he asked me to go to Washington on
his special train with his family, friends, and some members
of his new cabinet." [3]

A few days after the inauguration, Daniels called at the
White House with a recommendation that the Shipping
Board be abolished. He recalled to Roosevelt Wilson's remark that "all boards are long, wooden and narrow." Roosevelt accepted Daniels' recommendation with the comment
that "you have talked yourself out of a job." He told Daniels,
however, that he wouldn't be in Raleigh long because he
would soon be asked to come back.

Daniels had hardly reached his home after the inauguration
when he received a telephone call from Cordell Hull, the
new Secretary of State, saying that the President wished to
name Daniels Ambassador to Mexico. Undoubtedly Daniels
would have loved a Cabinet post, especially his old one as
Navy Secretary. But when Roosevelt became President,
Daniels was almost seventy-one. Seven years later, just before
war broke out in Europe and just after his seventy-seventh
birthday, Daniels wrote to Roosevelt from Mexico asking

---

3. Josephus Daniels, *Shirt-Sleeve Diplomat* (Chapel Hill, The University
of North Carolina Press, 1947), p. 16.

that he be named Secretary of the Navy, a suggestion Roosevelt did not take.

When Daniels told his wife of his call from Hull, she replied: "But you can't go to Mexico." She remembered the landing at Veracruz of April 21, 1914, ordered by Daniels on instruction from President Wilson. Daniels had forgotten for the moment that he signed the orders directing Rear Admiral Frank F. Fletcher to seize the custom house at Veracruz and to prevent war supplies from being delivered to the Huerta government. The landing resulted in the death of 126 Mexicans and the wounding of 195 others. The Mexicans had not forgotten.

While dining at the White House a short time after the announcement of Daniels' appointment to Mexico, Mrs. Daniels asked Roosevelt if he had not considered the Veracruz incident. Roosevelt was silent a moment. "I had forgotten all about the Veracruz incident," he replied. "Had the Chief?" [4]

4. Daniels, *Shirt-Sleeve Diplomat*, p. 5.

3

PRESIDENT AND AMBASSADOR

WASHINGTON, March 21, 1933

MEMORANDUM FOR HON. JOSEPHUS DANIELS

I have had dozens of letters of congratulations on your appointment to Mexico but I shall only send you those from "kickers." It is just as well to be able to separate the sheep from the goats! Here is the only objector so far—a pretty fine record.

F.D.R.

Roosevelt enclosed a telegram from Dr. M. J. Ferguson in Mexico City which said, "Why open old sore in Mexico's side appointing Josephus Daniels ambassador to Mexico?"

Typical of Daniels' broad human understanding and sympathy was his lack of resentment toward Dr. Ferguson for sending such a complaint to the President. Mrs. Ferguson and Mrs. Daniels met in Mexico City at a garden club and their husbands became friends. Daniels never told Dr. Ferguson that Roosevelt had sent him the telegram. "Once when I was taken painfully ill in the middle of the night with something that resembled ptomaine poisoning," Daniels recalled in *Shirt-*

Sleeve Diplomat, "Dr. Ferguson was summoned. He used the stringent remedies needed and remained until the cause had been removed. My wife, most anxious and distressed, had wanted, before calling Dr. Ferguson, to telephone her doctor son in Washington, Dr. Worth Bagley Daniels, but realized that long-distance treatment was not the urgent need. However, after Dr. Ferguson had 'brought me through' by what I called drastic methods, she said, 'And now I am going to call Worth by long distance.' It was for her own satisfaction after the tension. Dr. Ferguson said, 'Mrs. Daniels, your son probably has a hard day ahead of him. Why disturb his rest in the middle of the night and unfit him for his duties tomorrow?' But she felt it would calm and assure her if she could hear his voice. When she persisted Dr. Ferguson said, 'I pray you, Mrs. Daniels, don't be a damned fool.' That unexpected prescription both stunned and stopped her, and a hearty laugh removed the strain. The doctor's apologies were accepted. Ever after in the family and in the Embassy, if it was thought anyone was about to do something wholly unnecessary, the advice was, 'Follow Dr. Ferguson's prescription.' That, and 'Don't violate Rule No. 6—don't take yourself so damn seriously,' were the only standing orders in the Chancery and in the Embassy." [1]

WASHINGTON, March 1933

DEAR MR. PRESIDENT:

In the present financial crisis Legislatures in some States are in danger of reducing appropriations for universities and public schools to the point where the ills of depression will deny to youths the advantages which they sorely need.

President Graham, of the University of North Carolina,

---

1. Daniels, *Shirt-Sleeve Diplomat*, p. 388.

and others have requested me to express the hope that you could make a way to say something that could check this tide that would engulf the educational institutions. They suggest that in the World War, President Wilson urged the colleges to carry on, and expressed the hope that in this emergency you could find a way to warn against the danger of compelling youth to bear the burden of depression.

I am enclosing what Wilson said. At present I am seeking to familiarize myself with Mexican problems and will call to see you before leaving for Mexico City to receive instructions.

Faithfully yours,
Josephus Daniels

[Frank P. Graham (later United States Senator) was President of the University of North Carolina.]

Washington, March 27, 1933

Dear Chief:

When I get a chance I will say something about maintaining the work of the universities and schools. One of the difficulties is that most of the College Presidents and Commissioners of Education have been unwilling to cut costs in proportion to their enterprises. In most parts of the country the past decade has seen a very large increase in teachers' salaries, and even if all teachers were cut 15%, like government employees, they would still be getting relatively more than in 1914!

Always sincerely,
Franklin D. Roosevelt

[Daniels fought all his life for better schools, always a matter of great concern to Southern leaders like Daniels and

Graham. Roosevelt's reply could hardly have made Daniels happy, for the President's broad generalization about the pay of teachers was inaccurate as far as the South was concerned.]

NEW YORK, March 30, 1933

TELEGRAM TO ROOSEVELT

The best thing you have done is to strike a body blow to *caveat emptor*. That hoary old inciter of fraud has encumbered the stage too long. It is such acts that make me proud to call you chief. Warm regards.

JOSEPHUS DANIELS

[On March 29, 1933, Roosevelt sent a message to Congress recommending federal supervision of investment securities in interstate commerce. "This proposal," Roosevelt told Congress, "adds to the ancient rule of *caveat emptor*, the further doctrine 'let the seller also beware.' It puts the burden of telling the whole truth on the seller."]

MEXICO, April 18, 1933

DEAR FRANKLIN:

Agreeable to my promise to write you now and then something "off the record" about the duties, official and otherwise, to which you have assigned me, I am giving myself the pleasure of relating something of the first days since I told you good-bye, which may have an interest apart from my official reports....

We stayed in Raleigh, packing up our belongings (richer in things than we imagined), until Tuesday, April 11th, when more people than could get into the Union Station at Raleigh gathered to say good-bye and wish us well....

The secret service men who had been assigned to the Embassy remained with us until yesterday, when I, expressing deep appreciation of the consideration, requested that they be withdrawn, as I felt—and those of the Embassy staff felt—there was no need for them, and, as a matter of fact, their presence might indicate that we feared some of the imaginary things that had been published might take place.

You know, and I know, that there is no safety for any man in public life anywhere if there is in the hearts of men a desire to do him injury. It is important, of course, that secret service men should be employed to give every protection possible to the Chief Magistrate, but they did not save Lincoln, they did not save Garfield, and they did not save McKinley. The only way that a man in public life can be perfectly safe from any sort of attack is to be hermetically sealed in a water-tight compartment. I think it is better to run some risk than to die of such suffocation and fear. I do not think your wife ever said anything wiser than, after the attempt upon your life at Miami, when she was offered police escort, she declined it, saying that people in public life must know that they must expect whatever happened....

Please tell Mrs. Roosevelt that we are fully and happily counting upon her coming this summer, and have already selected the room for her, looking out upon a whole garden and wall of the most beautiful flowers she could imagine.

The only fly in the ointment here, and that is not a fly really, is that the distance makes it impossible for me to drop into the White House every few days and have a little controversy with you about whether I shall call you "chief" or you shall go back to the old days and call me "chief." The photograph which you inscribed so affectionately stands on the center table at the residence. As our goods have not arrived it is, in fact, our only Lares and Penates, and we regard that as very fitting....

Always affectionately yours,

JOSEPHUS DANIELS

[An attempt was made on Roosevelt's life in Miami in February, 1933.]

MEXICO, April 19, 1933

DEAR FRANKLIN (Easy Boss):

Of course you know, what was news to me, that this Ambassador for the time being holds a position somewhat like Mahomet's coffin—between the earth and the sky. He is an Ambassador so far as his own country is concerned, and part Ambassador toward Mexico. But he does not come fully out of the shell until he has been received by the President and has made his address to His Excellency. That function will take place probably next Monday or Tuesday. Until then, though I have presented my credentials and your letter to Dr. Jose Manuel Puig Casauranc, the Minister for Foreign Affairs, I am only a fifty-fifty Ambassador. I wonder if the other fifty is editor or an ovum. It is now expected at the Embassy that I will be received either next Monday or Tuesday.

I have written my address and when you read it, if you will do me that honor, you will find that it breathes the same spirit as characterized your address last week at the Pan American gathering. In fact, an expert in plagiarism might charge me with having appropriated some of your views and expressions. If so, all the better.

I find in diplomacy there is no such speed as has actuated the Administration at Washington since the 4th of March.

They take things more leisurely and give plenty of time for consideration. To men who believe in action, action, action, as we do, this at first seems a rather slow progress. I guess that the lack of speed insures more time for study, and results in fewer mistakes. And mistakes between our own country and another are much more to be avoided than when we are dealing with our own countrymen. They excuse mistakes if the result is satisfactory. However, diplomats are not expected to engage in experiments.

It may be that the postponement of my reception by the President until next week has some reference to the fact that on April 21st the Mexican Government is bestowing medals on certain of the defenders of Veracruz. While nothing has been said about it, or even hinted, there is a feeling at the Embassy that the Government would prefer not to have me presented on the day that the medals are given to the men who defended Veracruz when the marines and sailors were landed to take the customs house at that port, under orders which I issued as Secretary of the Navy.

Some attempt has been made, as you know, to stir up feeling about that. It surprised me very much, for, as you will remember, the only purpose on the part of President Wilson in causing that order to be issued was to prevent the landing of munitions from the *Ypiranga*, a German ship which was taking a large supply of munitions to Huerta, and which were to be delivered at Veracruz. Our only purpose was to keep these arms out of the hands of the Huerta forces, feeling that if the Huertistas should obtain these arms, they might be used to strengthen their position and weaken the position of President Wilson in refusing to grant recognition to Huerta. And even more so, as far as the United States was concerned, if these arms fell into the hands of the Huerta forces, they might be used against the forces under General Pershing, which had been sent into Northern Mexico....

Faithfully yours,

JOSEPHUS DANIELS

MEXICO, April 26, 1933

DEAR SENOR DON FRANKLIN D. ROOSEVELT,

I have sometimes wondered how a young chicken, confined in the egg shell, felt in the week prior to being emancipated from his dark home and coming into the light. At last I fully understand the feeling. For one week I have been that embryo chicken, neither egg nor fowl, Ambassador designate, but not having a leg to stand on.

Now that I was received yesterday afternoon, with the pomp and ceremony reminiscent of old Spanish grandeur, I feel pretty like an Ambassador Extraordinary and Plenipotentiary, though that mouth-filling phrase almost choked me when I uttered it in the Palace in the address I made to President Rodriguez, presenting your recall of Ambassador Clark (though he went to Utah before you named his successor) and my own letter of credence. It was all very grand and I felt, as Napoleon said in Egypt, "twenty centuries look down upon you." The palace is more than three hundred years old, of noble architecture, with magnificent large portraits of Benito Juarez and the other leaders of Mexican Independence and of former days....

The climate is ideal here and my wife and I are very happy. She joins me in love to you and Mrs. Roosevelt.

Afectuosamente, mi querido amigo y Presidente,

JOSEPHUS DANIELS

[Abelardo L. Rodríguez was President of Mexico from 1932 to 1934. Reuben Clark was Daniels' predecessor as Ambassador to Mexico.]

MEXICO, May 15, 1933

DEAR MR. PRESIDENT:

...I recall what you said about General Calles when I was in Washington. You sized him up right. He holds no official position but is the head of the National Revolutionary Party and all the public officials look up to him and lean upon him. There are two opinions about him—one that he is the real Boss who enjoys saying who shall or shall not hold office—a Mexican Warwick; the other, and the opinion held by Americans who seem to understand the Mexican situation, is that he put aside office because he is not personally ambitious, and is a patriot who sees that peace in Mexico is essential to its development and that in the present situation it can be had only through the Revolutionary Party, which is in fact the only strong party here. His admirers say that General Calles does not wish to name the next President (he named the present one, and Ortiz Rubio, and Portes Gil), but wishes to keep the Party strong because he fears if the Revolutionary Party loses control, peace will come to an end. I have not been here long enough to justify an opinion....

Some of the papers published that General Calles left Mexico City before I arrived because he was not pleased with the appointment. There was nothing in that. Isn't it strange how newspaper men (me with the rest) can imagine something and give it wings?...

Affectionately yours,

JOSEPHUS DANIELS

[Plutarco Elías Calles fought against the Huerta forces in 1913. He was President of Mexico from 1924 to 1928, when he was succeeded by Emilio Portes Gil. Calles continued to wield powerful influence over Mexican affairs as the real leader of the National Revolutionary party. In 1934 Calles helped elect Lázaro Cárdenas as President. They quarrelled, however, and in 1936 Cárdenas exiled Calles, who moved to California. Portes Gil was President from 1928 to 1930, Pascual Ortiz Rubio from 1930 to 1932, Rodríguez from 1932 to 1934 and Cárdenas from 1934 to 1940.]

MEXICO, June 1, 1933

DEAR FRANKLIN:

If I were to write you every time you do something that makes me wish to say "Bravo," you would not have time to do the big things that are characterizing your administration. Instead of taking up so much of your time, I drop a line now and then to some Senator or Representative congratulating the Democrats in Congress for standing firmly behind the progressive (should I not rather say revolutionary?) policies which have been set in motion since March 4th.

Some of my Congressional friends (only a few) have not been as enthusiastic as they should be. In fact, some of our Southern Democrats, who have been too near the power and high tariff influences than was wise, have had to gag several times before they swallowed the Roosevelt medicine. This was particularly true as to Muscle Shoals and regulation of industry. But most of them have swallowed it down and concealed their wry faces. . . .

In connection with the Morgan investigation, it seems fortunate that our friend Carter Glass is not Secretary of the

Treasury. He is able and honest and I hold him in high esteem. However, he is an individualist to the nth degree. In the Morgan matter, I think unconsciously he is influenced in his criticism of Pecora by his high regard for Mr. Leffingwell. You may recall that when Glass (then Secretary of the Treasury) resigned to accept appointment to the Senate, he urged Wilson to appoint Leffingwell as Secretary of the Treasury. He said that he was the best man for the place, and he is a high class man. I went to see Mr. Wilson and urged him to name a Democrat who was interested primarily in the success of his Administration and in the continuance of the Democratic Party in power. Glass was disappointed that Wilson did not accept his recommendations for Leffingwell, who later went with Morgan, thereby showing he was not deeply concerned with policies to put an end to favoritism or privilege. Glass knows nothing of team work, and it is better for him and for you that he remain where he feels team work is not required.

I am glad to see Senator Couzens is going to London as the Republican member. He has independence and courage, and wears no man's collar.

With my affectionate regards and congratulations on the great achievements of your Administration in its first few weeks, I am, as ever

Faithfully yours,
Josephus Daniels

No answer is expected. Submitted, in accordance with our understanding, for such consideration as it may justify.

J.D.

[Russell C. Leffingwell was Assistant Secretary of the Treasury from 1917 to 1920, when he resigned to join the

J. P. Morgan Company. Ferdinand Pecora was counsel to the Senate Committee on Banking and Currency when it conducted the investigation into banking and stock market practices in 1933 and 1934. Carter Glass, a friend of Daniels and Roosevelt, was Wilson's Secretary of the Treasury from December, 1918, to February, 1920, and a member of the Senate from Virginia from 1920 to his death in 1946. When Roosevelt was elected President, he offered Glass the Treasury portfolio, but Glass declined. It was not long before Glass was a leading critic of Roosevelt's fiscal policies. James Couzens, a liberal Republican, was Senator from Michigan from 1925 to 1936. He was a member of the United States delegation to the London Monetary Conference of 1933.]

DEAR FRANKLIN: June 13, 1933

When I picked up the paper yesterday and saw you had named Dodd as Ambassador to Germany and had called Ray Stevens and John Fahey to your aid in important positions (to name the three of your good appointments I know best) I wished I could take wings and fly over the White House (not as Gabriel but as a Jonathan) and tell you how such appointments are sure to hearten the country and insure the carrying out of truly progressive policies.

Dodd was born near Raleigh and we are old friends. One of these days he will write the best book of this Era of Revolution by peaceful methods.

My wife joins me in love to Mrs. Roosevelt. You both know that in all things that touch you or your heart, we are in accord and affection.

Faithfully,
JOSEPHUS DANIELS

[Roosevelt appointed William E. Dodd as Ambassador to Germany, Raymond B. Stevens a member of the Federal Trade Commission, and John H. Fahey as chairman of the Federal Home Loan Bank Board.]

MEXICO, July 10, 1933

MY DEAR CHIEF:

Knowing that you were under too great a strain to read anything except the most important and pressing documents bearing upon the work of Congress during its last days and the putting of its grants of large power in operation, plus the exigencies of the World Economic Conference problems, I have of late neglected my promise to keep you advised of what is going on in this neighboring country. In comparison with the issues of tremendous importance at Washington and London, I recognize that what concerns the Embassy here is not of great importance....

The only thing that stands out here above every other influence confirms what you told me just before I left Washington, to wit, that General Calles is "the big boy" of Mexico. He has no official status (his only public position is President of the Board of Directors of the National Railways of Mexico, and also of course his rank in the army, his present status being Divisional General on waiting order status), but all officialdom "kowtows" to "the General", as he is called. There are plenty of Generals in Mexico (376 with an army of 53,000, whereas we have 67 with an army of 130,000)....

When the Japanese owners of berry farms in California reduced the wages of Mexican berry pickers to starvation wages, it was General Calles who made direct appeal to

Governor Rolph in behalf of the Mexicans. When the strike against starvation wages occurred, and the places of the Mexican workers were taken by Japanese children of under age, Dr. Puig, Minister for Foreign Affairs, spoke to me about it and the hardship it entailed on Mexicans living in the United States. I at once called the matter to the attention of the State Department and requested that the appeal of the Mexican Government be brought to the attention of Governor Rolph. Of course I knew the Federal Government could not act in any direct manner, but that, as in the Japanese ownership of land in the Wilson administration, the Secretary of State could bring it to the attention of the Governor of California. He did so. About that time General Johnson had secured the cooperation of the textile manufacturers to agree to cut out child labor, and as the Japanese were using child labor, the situation was cleared up by withdrawing the Japanese children from the berry fields and giving the Mexican workers a living wage. This incident created the greatest interest here and the papers were full of it, rejoicing when the strike was happily ended. Dr. Puig appreciated our cooperation. I was advised by some Americans here to tell the Foreign Minister I could not even bring the matter to the attention of our Government. That is not my idea of my duty. The call to humanity transcends red tape or archaic diplomatic side stepping...

　With my affectionate regards to you and Mrs. Roosevelt,

Faithfully yours,

JD

　[James Rolph, Jr., was Governor of California. Brigadier General Hugh S. Johnson was administrator of the National Recovery Administration.]

MEXICO, July 26, 1933

DEAR FRANKLIN:

I have been having some correspondence with Roy Howard with reference to the telegram which he sent out from Brest telling of the Armistice before it had been signed. Closing his letter he says:

"Felicitating you upon your infinitely greater wisdom than my own as regards Frank Roosevelt, who has proved one of the happiest surprises of my life."

He made this reference doubtless because some time before the Chicago Convention I talked with him. He was then enthusiastic for Smith and was so strong for him he could not do you justice. It must gratify you to see how such critics have now become warm supporters.

Faithfully yours,

JD

[It was not long, of course, before Roy Howard, publisher of the Scripps-Howard papers, joined the ranks of the most bitter Roosevelt critics.]

The following letter from Daniels was sent by President Roosevelt to Secretary of State Hull with this note: "I think you will be interested in this letter from Mr. Daniels. FDR." A week later it was returned by Hull to the President: "I return, herewith, Ambassador Daniels' letter which I have read with a great deal of interest. Many thanks for bringing it to my attention. C.H."

MEXICO, September 9, 1933

DEAR CHIEF:

I have tried to keep the State Department in touch with Latin American sentiment here with reference to the Cuban

situation. It is difficult for the average American at home
to understand the deep-seated resentment of action by our
government in the countries south of the Rio Grande. These
people—or most of them—act in accordance with the statement often made that our application of the Monroe Doctrine is that we have denied to any European country the
right to secure territory or dominion on this hemisphere
because we wish that exclusive right for ourselves. They have
long memories. If it is pointed out that the United States
is actuated solely as a neighbor who wishes to help in stable
government, those who are not as polite as most Latin
Americans answer with a sneer: "What about the rape of a
large part of the Mexican territory after the war in 1846?"
or "That does not comport with the forced Gadsden treaty
by which Mexico lost more territory." They still remember
with resentment Pershing's expedition, the Tampico incident,
and the "taking" of Veracruz. Of course as to the events
under Wilson, the ablest will admit that while Wilson may
have had no right to send troops or sailors to Mexican territory, his action helped to rid Mexico of the unspeakable
Huerta. Nobody has a good word for him. Next to him the
most despised man of that era is Henry Lane Wilson. Leading
people here accuse Ambassador Wilson of moral responsibility
for the murder of Madero. I am quite sure (and his own
reports support this belief) that he had large part in extorting
the resignation of Madero when Huerta betrayed him. Wilson and Huerta were intimates, drank together, and Wilson
did nothing to save Madero's life though Mrs. Madero begged
him to do so. His egotism led to his helping to set up the
Huerta Government. Also his close relations with foreign
owners of valuable property who wished a tool like Huerta

or American intervention and annexation of Mexico to the United States.

But all that is a long story and I have learned many things of those tragic days that make one ashamed of his countrymen. We have had too much Dollar Diplomacy on this hemisphere. Latin Americans resent our long occupation of Haiti and Nicaragua, our sending Marines to Nicaragua, our virtual dictatorship (as they allege) in Central America, but, most of all, they grow red when talking about how your Uncle Ted "took" Panama while Congress was talking. Many of them believe we have avid eyes on Havana and would rejoice at a reasonable excuse to annex it. They recognize that "the Colossus of the North" could annex Mexico, Cuba and Central America by its superior strength. Some of them cannot understand how any man or nation can fail to grab if they have the power. This class thinks we are only awaiting a good opportunity to take weak countries which our financiers could better exploit by the aid of Marine occupation. . . .

If the worst comes to the worst (in Cuba)—and I hope and pray it may not—I have written Hull strongly urging that we act in concert with Mexico and the A.B.C. powers to restore order and help to set up a stable government. Such united action would remove the sting. Wilson waited too long to invite A.B.C. participation.

There is great confidence here in Government circles and in the Diplomatic Corps that you will handle the Cuban situation wisely. I pray you may have guidance in a delicate and difficult situation.

Faithfully yours,
JOSEPHUS DANIELS

[Henry Lane Wilson was Ambassador to Mexico when Woodrow Wilson became President. About two weeks before the inauguration of Wilson, President Francisco I. Madero and Vice President Pino Suárez were murdered by Victoriano Huerta's men. Madero was a popular and pro-democratic leader feared by Huerta and his reactionary supporters. The A.B.C. powers are Argentina, Brazil, and Chile.]

WASHINGTON, November 10, 1933

MY DEAR MR. DANIELS:

As the year draws to a holiday pause before its close, I take much pleasure in sending out to you and through you to your personal and official family, and to the Foreign Service staffs in Mexico, my heartiest good wishes. Your loyal and intelligent cooperation with us in Washington has made these recent months of our association a source of great satisfaction and encouragement to me in this important period of our country's development.

In offering my best greetings for Christmas and the New Year, I look forward in confident anticipation to continuing mutual cooperation during 1934.

Very sincerely yours,

FRANKLIN D. ROOSEVELT

[This was obviously a form letter sent to all American overseas missions. As will be noted in the next letter, it was another Roosevelt precedent.]

MEXICO, December 13, 1933

DEAR MR. PRESIDENT:

At a regular weekly meeting of the Staff—composed of all the commissioned officers of the Consulate General and

Commercial Attache's office, as well as of the Embassy—this morning, I read your gracious letter containing holiday greetings and good wishes for the New Year.

One of the oldest members of the Consulate staff said: "I have been in the service for many years and this is the first time a President ever sent us Christmas greetings and thanks for our cooperation. It heartens us to know that our superior in the White House recognizes our cooperative efforts and sends us his appreciation."

I feel sure that it will gratify you to know that this thoughtful letter of appreciation warmed the hearts of all officers here, as it doubtless will in the remotest section of the world where Americans are serving under your administration.

I add my own thanks, and assurance of cooperation, to those of my colleagues.

Sincerely yours,

JOSEPHUS DANIELS

WASHINGTON, February 5, 1934

DEAR CHIEF:

It has been fairly definitely established that the fleet review will take place off Sandy Hook on Thursday, May thirty-first. As you know this will mark the return of the fleet to the Atlantic Coast after an absence of over three years.

In case there is any possibility of your being home at that time, it would be grand if you and Mrs. Daniels could join me at the review. Somehow I can think of nothing more wonderful than to have you standing beside me when the fleet goes by.

All goes well here and I have distinct hopes that the Congress will adjourn by the early part of May. If every thing else is quiet I hope that I can leave on a cruiser towards the end of June and go via Puerto Rico, Virgin Islands, and the Canal to Hawaii and the West Coast. In the old days you stole a march on me for I never got as far as the Hawaiian Islands!

Many thanks for that delightful birthday telegram.

Affectionately yours,

FRANKLIN D. ROOSEVELT

MEXICO, February 16, 1934

MY DEAR CHIEF:

My answer to the most appreciated order I have ever received, as contained in your letter of February 5th, is "Aye, Aye, sir." I assure you that no sailor ever uttered a more cheerful "Aye, Aye, sir" than is mine. Nothing could make me happier than to join you at the review of the Atlantic Fleet off Sandy Hook on the thirty-first of May....

Affectionately,

JOSEPHUS DANIELS

[Roosevelt and Daniels reviewed the fleet together off Sandy Hook on May 31. They had last reviewed the fleet together in 1918.]

MEXICO, March 14, 1934

DEAR FRANKLIN:

I had on my mind when in Washington to unbosom myself about a matter which had long been on my mind, but you were confronted with so many bigger things that I refrained. Now that aviation is to the fore, I wish to present for such consideration as you deem wise or conditions justify, the following:

You will remember that two years or so ago Representative Byrnes, of Tennessee, proposed to unite the departments of the Navy and Army under a Secretary of National Defense. I had some communication at that time with him and Speaker Garner and urged such action. It failed. Most Army and Navy Officers and their friends never change anything, as you know, that might alter their status if they can help it. If there are any reforms they must come from civilians aided by some broad-minded officers.

Recent events have convinced me that the suggestion of a Secretary of National Defense ought to unite both arms of the military service. Of course he would need to be a strong man, who knows something of the necessity for preparedness, ready to drastically end the overlapping and extravagance which inhere in both departments. In war, the Army and Navy must work together. They do not do it as effectively—indeed they cannot—as if they were united in peace and trained for acting as one strong right arm of the republic. . . .

When I was Secretary of the Navy I became convinced that the chasm which separates the two arms of the service ought to be bridged. Efficiency and economy alike demanded close cooperation. I advised a few plans for united action and presented them to Secretary Garrison. You know he was an outstanding rugged individualist who would have been horrified at the things you are doing.

"No use," he said, "to go into your suggestions. I don't care a damn about the Navy and you don't care a damn about the Army. You run your show and I will run mine." And we did, but cooperation would have made for economy and efficiency. . . .

Affectionately,

JOSEPHUS DANIELS

[Joseph W. Byrnes, of Tennessee, was Democratic leader of the House of Representatives from 1933 to 1935 and Speaker of the House from 1935 to his death in 1936. John N. Garner of Texas was Speaker of the House from 1931 to 1933 and Vice President from 1933 to 1941. Lindley M. Garrison was Secretary of War from 1913 to 1916.]

Daniels frequently alluded to the need for unification of the armed services. But not until after World War II, in the Truman administration, was unification achieved and the Department of Defense established. Roosevelt was not so strong in support of the idea as Daniels; yet the first American experience in World War II, at Pearl Harbor, showed that unity of command at least, which was achieved eventually in many theatres of the war, was vitally necessary.

MEXICO, July 28, 1934

DEAR FRANKLIN:

On my last visit to you in the White House, shortly before you left for Hawaii, you said: "Continue to write me letters about what you are thinking of." I am, therefore, complying, even at the risk of taking your thoughts from the most pressing matters.

I strongly believe we shall not solve the modern need until we abolish the Army and Navy portfolios and combine them under a Secretary of National Defense, and I believe we should have a Minister of Aviation to embrace flying of all kinds. Evidently the Baker board feels the strength of that argument, for it goes out of its way (as it seems to me) to stress its opposition to a consolidation of the aviation forces of the Government "into a Department of the Air or into a division of a new Department of National Defense as has been proposed." They base their opposition on "the ground of expense and of military efficiency." Upon the ground of expense, large savings could be effected by a unified air service. We now have one in the Army, the Navy, the Marine Corps, the Department of Commerce, and I do not know in how many more departments. The duplication and division is costly and experience shows has not made for efficiency. "Military efficiency" would in fact be promoted by a unified air service. . . .

I may be all wrong. Particularly, owing to more important matters, the time may not be propitious to undertaking these sweeping changes. If you undertook all these changes now, you might, in view of other immediate reforms that press for solution, be digging up more snakes than you could kill. But the sooner we have a unified air service, the better.

Faithfully yours,
JOSEPHUS DANIELS

[On July 18, 1934, a War Department special commission headed by former Secretary of War Newton D. Baker recommended against establishing a separate air force.]

Daniels continued to write very long letters to Roosevelt about nearly everything that happened. He went into great detail about such matters as claims, a radio conference, silver, etc. Some of these letters are omitted.

MEXICO, October 11, 1934

DEAR FRANKLIN:

Our friend McAdoo spent a couple of days here last week, coming in his plane "The Blue Streak." In the course of our talks I told him that I had expected him to be a leading champion of the New Deal measures in the Senate and I hoped, with the opening of the new Congress, he would take a more active part in combatting the attempts of the miners and sappers to weaken the recovery legislation. He is of the opinion that sentiment in the country is stronger for progressive—even constructively radical—legislation and administration than last year and favors going even further than the policies so far undertaken.

I am too far away from home to make me confident of my opinion about public sentiment in our country, but I told Raymond Moley when he was here that we should go further to the left rather than listen to the journals (which voice the views of Big Business) urging a reversal of policy. . . .

I told McAdoo that I had regretted to see him on several occasions side with Carter Glass, who is obsessed with the idea that the Federal Reserve Act, of which Carter thinks he is the sole author, makes no other legislation whatever necessary, when Carter was voting against and almost sneering at some essential New Deal policies. I knew I would hit him on the raw when I said Carter claimed to be "solely responsible for the Federal Reserve Act." McAdoo in his book gives account of his participation in securing that legislation and thinks he had an important part to play. And he did, but Carter, next to Woodrow Wilson, deserves the most credit. "There's glory enough to go round." Carter's mind is both closed and sealed to new ideas. . . .

Faithfully yours,

JD

[McAdoo was never an enthusiastic New Dealer and his relations with Roosevelt while F.D.R. was President were never intimate. But, as a Senator from California from 1933 to 1939, he supported administration leaders on some important issues. Raymond Moley, a New Deal braintruster, broke with F.D.R. early in the first term.]

WASHINGTON, November 19, 1934

MY DEAR MR. DANIELS:

Toward the close of my second year in office, I send to you and to the members of the Foreign Service in the country of your residence, as well as to your family, personal and official, my cordial Christmas and New Year's greetings.

I want all of you to know that in spite of the distance which separates you from the National Capital, you are often in my thoughts. We in the United States appreciate the service which all of you are giving to your country.

In a time of great difficulties in almost every part of the world, we are proud of the American Foreign Service. Once more I send you my warm greetings.

Very sincerely yours,

FRANKLIN D. ROOSEVELT

WASHINGTON, January 3, 1935

DEAR CHIEF:

I am sorry to send you this typewritten letter but I want you to know how much I appreciate the interesting ash tray. It sits on the table beside my chair in my study and I am really enjoying it.

My best to you all for the New Year.

Affectionately,

FRANKLIN D. ROOSEVELT

WASHINGTON, March 1, 1935

DEAR CHIEF:

It is literally true that I cannot even give thought to summer plans and I think you can so inform the Foreign Office. I have always wanted to visit Mexico but this particular year it is possible that the session of the Congress will last into the summer and, in any event, I shall probably be so much in need of complete relaxation after adjournment that I shall seek absolute quiet by going on board ship again and avoiding, if possible, all visits and official ceremonies.

The Senate, as you know by this time, is a complete and absurd mess. The big Work Relief Bill is only one item. They will get into similar absurdities and ill-considered positions on the N.R.A. extension legislation, on social insurance, on aviation, on shipping, on bonus, and probably a half a dozen other choice subjects. I am saying very little, keeping my temper and letting them literally stew in their own juice. I think it is the best policy for a while, and, incidentally, I hope that the Longs and others will stub their toes. This is, of course, a very difficult year, for we are past the emergency legislation and seeking to improve or make permanent many things which could not possibly have succeeded two years ago.

As ever yours,

F.D.R.

[Daniels had forwarded to Roosevelt on February 19 an official invitation to visit Mexico. This letter reflects Roosevelt's increasing annoyance with Congress, which in 1935 was just beginning to demonstrate its independence of the President. Relations between Roosevelt and Congress, despite the large Democratic majorities, were to go from bad to worse. Huey P. Long was Senator from Louisiana.]

MEXICO, April 4, 1935

DEAR FRANKLIN:

As you were away from Washington at the time Barney Baruch testified before the Nye Committee, I am calling your attention to the following extract from his testimony, which is enough to justify both of us patting ourselves on the back:

"In the early stages of the war there was no program in the Army. They did not even know what materials were necessary to equip the Army. There were about ten procurement divisions, each competing with the other. On the other hand, the Navy was well organized."

I have always been proud that we had no additional Assistant Secretary during the World War, but carried on without any change whatever in the organization, expanding along lines mapped out before the declaration of war, or adopted to meet the exigencies as demanded.

My wife joins in love to Mrs. Roosevelt.

Affectionately,

JOSEPHUS DANIELS

[Bernard M. Baruch was Chairman of the War Industries Board in World War I. Baruch and Daniels were old friends, despite their different backgrounds and points of view. In a letter to this writer, Baruch said: "I think Daniels was as responsible as anybody else for my being made Chairman of the War Industries Board, which rather surprised everybody because he was supposed to be against any man from Wall Street. I was a great admirer of Josephus Daniels—extraordinary man."]

WASHINGTON, July 12, 1935

DEAR CHIEF:

I have put off writing to you from time to time but I am sure you know we were all thinking of you and Mrs. Daniels after we heard of that bomb explosion in your garden. Your whole conduct was grand.

The general situation is, I well realize, confusing and difficult to forecast in regard to future events. I have had a talk with the Knights of Columbus people and with a number of others who wish to "resolve," start conferences, etc., etc. I think they see the danger to Catholics and to future relations if we Yankees start telling the Mexicans what to do.

I have been having a busy time, as you know, and the Congress got a bit obstreperous but they are going along better this week.

As ever yours,
FRANKLIN D. ROOSEVELT

[A bomb was exploded in the Embassy garden in the early summer, but it did no damage. Daniels was not perturbed. "Evidently the person who threw it, far from any building and just over the fence, wished merely to create a sensation or a fear," Daniels wrote to F.D.R. "In either case he was mistaken. Everything here is quiet."]

HYDE PARK, Nov. 1, 1935

DEAR CHIEF:

I have been tremendously interested in Mr. Jaime Gurza's book [*Logic, Roosevelt and the American People*]. I particularly like his clarity of expression and analysis in discussing our problems, and I am inclined to think that if his book were published in this country it might succeed and do good.

The trip on the *Houston* was a complete success—I have had plenty of sleep and exercise and we had some excellent fishing.

Now I am at Hyde Park for a week over Election Day and will go to Warm Springs about November twentieth for two weeks.

There is little news except the general thought that economic conditions are vastly better. I think people are getting tired of the attitude of Hearst, the Republican leaders and the old Wall Street crowd.

As ever yours,
Franklin D. Roosevelt

[In the fall of 1935, Roosevelt sailed on the cruiser *Houston* down the West Coast, through the Panama Canal, then north to Charleston, S. C.]

Warm Springs, Ga., November 27, 1935

My dear Mr. Ambassador:

The disturbed condition of world affairs during the year which is coming to a close has caused a measurable increase in your labors in protecting American interests, and I appreciate the distinguished service which you have rendered in this connection. I am grateful for the thorough manner in which you have kept me informed of developments abroad, and the counsel which you have supplied has been of great value to me.

I wish to send this word of appreciation and encouragement, together with my best wishes for Christmas and the New Year, to you and your family and to the officers and employees under your jurisdiction.

Sincerely yours,
Franklin D. Roosevelt

Washington, January 1, 1936

Dear Franklin:

Here is an expression from Holmes which, if it has missed you, is so good you may find a use for it in one of your "fireside" talks. Holmes said: "I find the great thing in the world is not so much where we stand, as in what direction we are moving. To reach the port of heaven we must sail sometimes with the wind and sometimes against it; but we must sail and not drift, nor lie at anchor."—New Year greetings to you and Mrs. Roosevelt.

Faithfully,
JOSEPHUS DANIELS

MEXICO, February 1, 1936

DEAR FRANKLIN:

It may be that you have not read Mark Sullivan's account of the propaganda against Theodore Roosevelt when he was fighting the "malefactors of great wealth." If not, or if you have forgotten, I am sure you will be interested in reading the enclosed. When I was in Washington at the Jackson Day dinner I saw Mark and reminded him of the days when he was a progressive and we were fighting together against the reactionaries, and told him I had come to Washington to summon him to come back to the colors. I rather think that he believed Hoover was a liberal at first and then became so closely associated with him and had such regard for his industry and integrity that he was swallowed up and of course flattered that Hoover leaned on him.

Privilege never surrenders and its devotees always follow the same rule. They are saying about you now what they said about Jefferson and Jackson and Theodore Roosevelt when he became a progressive.

With warm regards,

Faithfully yours,
JD

[Mark Sullivan, the newspaper columnist and author of *Our Times*, was a close friend of President Hoover.]

Los Angeles, Calif., February 15, 1936

Dear Franklin:

I thank you for the privilege of representing our Government at the San Diego Exposition. It enabled me to see the completion of the big naval centre we started in 1913-21 and meet old friends. Your message was enthusiastically received.

It made me very happy to note the wonderful impression you made on your trip here last fall. It abides. Its first fruit is that for the first time in history the registration in San Diego shows a very large Democratic majority. The same thing is true in Los Angeles. The Democrats are 6 to 7 of the Republican registration. The people are for you and in spite of some inside party divisions they will vote for you in November....

I am distressed to hear of the illness of our friend Claude Swanson and hope he is on the road to improvement.

Affectionately yours,
JOSEPHUS DANIELS

[Claude Swanson was Secretary of the Navy from 1933 to 1939.]

Washington, February 27, 1936

Dear Chief:

It is good to have your note from Los Angeles and I am happy to know that you found things in good shape in southern California.

We are deeply distressed about Harry Roosevelt. He was an excellent Assistant Secretary and Claude Swanson leaned on him heavily. The latter is making an amazing recovery. A week ago we thought there was no chance of his pulling through. I saw him on Thursday last and though he was very weak he had all the old light of battle in his eyes, and is, I think, going to get well by sheer will power.

Affectionately,
FRANKLIN D. ROOSEVELT

[Henry Latrobe Roosevelt, a distant cousin of F.D.R., was Assistant Secretary of the Navy from 1933 until his death on February 22, 1936.]

MEXICO, April 30, 1936

DEAR FRANKLIN:

I was very glad to read yesterday in the San Antonio paper that at your press conference you had stated that you favored action at the Democratic National Convention in Philadelphia looking to the abolition of the archaic two-thirds rule required for the nomination of President and Vice President. I was happy to see this because I had lost hope of having the rule repealed in any convention where there is a strong contest for the nomination. This year it will all be plain sailing and you will be nominated virtually by acclamation, and the "changing the rules during the game," of which we heard so much in Chicago in 1932, cannot be brought forward....

As you know, this rule was forced upon the party in the old days of the slavery and anti-slavery agitation, when the South had enough influence in the Democratic Party to impose its will, and the Southern leaders demanded that they be allowed a veto for the nomination of any man, and they could obtain the veto only by the two-thirds rule. Insistence upon that rule more than anything else caused a division in the Democratic ranks in 1860 and put the party out of power for half a century. Ten years ago I secured the adoption of a resolution at the State Convention in North Carolina for the abolition of the two-thirds rule and I am glad to be living and in fine fettle to see this anachronism ended. . . .

Affectionately yours,
JOSEPHUS DANIELS

[The two-thirds rule was abolished, despite considerable Southern opposition, at the Democratic National Convention in 1936. In the 1932 convention Roosevelt had a simple majority on the first ballot, but it was not until the fourth ballot that he received the necessary two-thirds vote. If the simple majority rule had prevailed in 1912, Champ Clark of Missouri would have been nominated on the tenth ballot instead of Woodrow Wilson on the forty-sixth. In June, 1936, at the Democratic National Convention in Philadelphia, Roosevelt was renominated on the first ballot.]

ABOARD THE SCHOONER YACHT Sewanna
July 19, 1936

DEAR CHIEF:

Two delightful letters from you have come to me here off the coast of Nova Scotia where I am re-living some of my boyhood days on a small schooner.

Will you tell the Mexican Postmaster General how happy I am at the thought of finding the set of commemorative stamps when I get back to Washington? I will write him in person.

I am delighted that the opening of the highway to Mexico City was such a success and that the V.P. made such a splendid impression. In this connection, I think it would really pay the Mexican Government to do a little advertising of this highway, for the very good reason that there has been on the whole little publicity about this opening and thousands of automobile tourists would use it if they knew about it. Even a small advertising appropriation of perhaps $25,000 would bring lots of results but the ad ought to be sure to mention adequate hotel facilities between the U. S. border and Mexico City and also reasonable prices.

I expect to have a campaignless August and September—two inspection trips into the flood areas of New England, New York and Pennsylvania and a two-weeks trip starting in the drought area of the Dakotas and then down the Mississippi River from St. Paul to Memphis and back to Washington via the Great Smokies, Tennessee and North Carolina. Don't you think this is a good idea, especially if I can talk of natural resources and avoid all political speeches? I am inclined to think that the Republican high command is shooting off all their ammunition too soon and that people will be rather sick of their same old story by the end of September.

As ever yours,

Franklin D. Roosevelt

Mexico, July 27, 1936

Dear Franklin:

I was very happy to get your letter and glad that you took time from fishing while aboard the schooner yacht *Sewanna* to write me about your plans for August and September. I cannot imagine where you got the new way of spelling *Sewanee*. I thought the only way of spelling it was *Sewanee*, but I guess that is the southern way and your way is the Yankee way....

I think the trip you have outlined is the best employment of your time that you can make in August and part of September. ...While you are making these addresses, however, I am strongly of the opinion that we ought not to let August pass without effective replies to the attempts of our opponents to ride into office by promising to do some of the things you have already done and permitting the people to forget that they were in power for twelve years and did not turn a hand to end unemployment or to lift the farmers out of the slough of despond.... You and I by experience know what a tough old bird the Republican Party is ... with the unlimited money at its disposal....

Faithfully yours,
JOSPEHUS DANIELS

MEXICO, August 21, 1936

DEAR FRANKLIN:

The church situation has improved somewhat. There has been no active persecution and President Cardenas has several times told me that there will be none. I have tried to impress upon him our American point of view.

Frank Tannenbaum, of Columbia University faculty, who knows Mexico better than any man except Ernest Gruening, spent two weeks with President Cardenas on a recent trip over the new highway. He has his confidence and General C. talks freely with him. I told Frank that the fact that no Catholic churches were open in Veracruz, Sonora and some other states injured the prestige of Mexico and he ought to say so to President Cardenas. He could do it wholly unofficially....

Affectionately,
JOSEPHUS DANIELS

[Frank Tannenbaum, a prolific writer on Latin America, was a frequent visitor to Mexico. Ernest Gruening was Director of the Division of Territories and Island Possessions of the Department of the Interior from 1934 to 1939, when he was appointed Governor of Alaska.]

MEXICO, September 28, 1936

DEAR FRANKLIN:

Nothing has cheered me more than your letter to Senator Bankhead and your statement in the press of your purpose to study the best means of decreasing farm tenancy in this country. . . . In December, before Wilson was inaugurated, visiting him at Trenton, I ventured to tell him that the biggest opportunity of his administration was in securing better prices for farm products and lifting agriculture out of the depths. I told him that the most important member of his Cabinet was his Secretary of Agriculture, who should devote himself to a radical departure from the old ways.

"You are right," he said, "and I have selected the very man as Secretary of Agriculture to do the things we both agree are of the highest importance."

And then he named Houston!—a scholar and economist of the oldest and most archaic school—and we both know that he had neither a new idea nor sympathy with the tenants and struggling farmers.

More power to your arm in this great adventure for the Forgotten Man, the most miserable and hopeless of all our countrymen! . . .

My stay in Mexico has taught me the real reason for the poverty of the people and the backwardness of the country. From the days of Cortez until the expulsion of Diaz there was no such thing in Mexico as farmers who owned and worked their own farms. As you know the *Conquistadores* divided the country among themselves under a system of *encomiendas*, every hacienda being composed of thousands of acres of land with enough Indians to work it. The Indian workers in most instances were little less than slaves, without the protection and consideration slaves enjoyed on most plantations. . . . At the end of the rule of Diaz two per cent of the population owned seventy per cent of the land. . . .

If tenancy continues to go forward by leaps and bounds in our country the time will come when peonage will be the curse of the United States as it has been of Mexico and Ireland. You will avert this tragedy by securing just methods by which tenants may be aided to own the land they till.

- With my sincere regards and rejoicing in all you are doing to lift our country to higher planes,

Affectionately yours,
JOSEPHUS DANIELS

[Roosevelt, on September 21, 1936, asked Senator John H. Bankhead of Alabama and Representative Marvin Jones of Texas to prepare a federal plan to attack the farm tenancy problem. David F. Houston was Secretary of Agriculture from 1913 to 1920.}

WASHINGTON, November 9, 1936

DEAR CHIEF:

I am beginning to come up for air after the baptism on Tuesday night last! The other fellow was the one who nearly drowned.

Thank the Lord it was not a close vote or even a gain for Brother Landon over what Herbert Hoover got in 1932. If Landon had got the 120 or 130 votes in the electoral college as most dispassionate observers, including Emil Hurja, thought he would get, the reactionary element would have used that fact everlastingly during the next two years.

We have—all of us—been leaning over backward in taking the general victory calmly and in asserting that there will be no reprisals.

Nevertheless, the campaign, as Jim Farley predicted in June, was a dirty one, but I am thankful that the dirt was about 99 per cent on the Republican side, including, of course, the Coughlin and Liberty League and "Jeffersonian Democrats" outfits, all of them without doubt financed with the full knowledge and approval of ————.

One of the most amazing of the undoubted facts of the campaign was the discrediting not only of the Hearst papers, the Chicago *Tribune*, the New York *Herald Tribune* and *Sun* and the Boston *Herald*, but also of dozens of smaller papers which aped the others in coloring every news story and crowding their editorials with every known form of misrepresentation. As a matter of fact I think this type of newspaper so overdid things that the public saw through it at least by September and since then the attacks gained us votes. The same thought applies to the attack on the Social Security Act in the last two weeks of the campaign. It was so obviously untrue and unfair that we were helped.

My greatest regret of the whole campaign was that you could not have been in the thick of the fray yourself, and I missed you much....

If the shipping strike is in a fair way to being settled, I shall leave the seventeenth and go to Buenos Aires at twenty-five knots an hour. Again, I wish you could be with me.

Love to you both,

Affectionately,

FRANKLIN D. ROOSEVELT

[Roosevelt's victory on November third over Alf M. Landon was by an even larger margin than his victory over Herbert Hoover four years earlier. Emil Hurja, a statistician for the Democratic National Committee, had predicted a much closer race. About 85 per cent of the press was against Roosevelt's bid for a second term. His increasing annoyance with the press is reflected in many letters to Daniels. On November 18, Roosevelt sailed from Charleston on the Cruiser *Indianapolis* for a cruise to Buenos Aires.]

MEXICO, January 20, 1937

TELEGRAM TO ROOSEVELT

My heart swelled with pride at your magnificent dedication to carry on and bring justice and comfort to those denied their rightful blessings. We heard you perfectly at the Embassy. I ardently wished there was some way by which I could transmit the glorious sunshine that floods this city today.

Affectionately,

JOSEPHUS DANIELS

[Roosevelt was inaugurated for a second term on January 20, 1937.]

WASHINGTON, January 22, 1937

DEAR CHIEF:

It was very delightful to receive that fine message you sent me, and I want you to know how gratified I am that you think so well of my Second Inaugural Address. Ever so many thanks for letting me know of your approval.

A little of your sunshine would have been welcome. But your messages always warm the heart!

Very sincerely yours,

F.D.R.

MEXICO, Feb. 5, 1937

TELEGRAM TO ROOSEVELT

The spirit of Thomas Jefferson and Old Hickory are hovering over the White House. If those who have gone before know what is transpiring in this sphere Jefferson and Jackson "bravo" when your message was carried on the celestial broadcast. More power to your arm in cutting the judicial Gordian knot.

JOSEPHUS DANIELS

[Roosevelt's controversial proposal to reorganize and enlarge the Supreme Court was sent to Congress on February 5, 1937.]

WASHINGTON, February 8, 1937

DEAR CHIEF:

It was good to get your telegram the other day and I wish you were here to see the way the conservatives are running around tearing their hair and using language about me which surpasses even that of the campaign. . . .

As ever yours,

F.D.R.

WASHINGTON, October 7, 1937

DEAR CHIEF:

I put to good use those two delightful stories you wrote me.

This has been a wonderful trip and has, I think, been productive of much good even in the East because the newspapermen, who nearly all represent "fat-cat" hostile papers, have had to comment on the crowds and the enthusiasm.

As ever yours,

FRANKLIN D. ROOSEVELT

Enclosed in Roosevelt's letter was the text of the informal remarks he had made at Fargo, N. D., on October 4, 1937. He said he wished "the calamity howlers and narrow-minded stay-at-homes could have gone across the continent" with him. If more people would get around the country, they would be more national in their point of view, he said, and added: "I remember a story that President Wilson told about North Dakota. He and his family, when he was President of Princeton, were spending the summer in England and one Sunday morning they went to church. The rector of the church got up and said, " 'The Bishop of North Dakota will preach today. We are to have the pleasure of having a sermon from the Bishop of North Dakota and, by way of explanation, let me tell you that North Dakota is one of His Majesty's colonies.'

"I heard another story the other day in a letter from the American Ambassador in Mexico City, Josephus Daniels. One day he got a letter from a friend of his in Chicago, who wrote, 'I'm contemplating a business trip to Mexico City. Do you think it would be safe for me to come and bring my wife and daughter with me?' A few hours later a Mexican friend of his came to the Embassy and said, 'Mr. Ambassador, I would like to go to the Chicago Exposition. Do you think it would be safe for me to take my wife and family to Chicago?' "

HYDE PARK, November 5, 1937

DEAR CHIEF:

I am glad you sent me the copy of your letter to Claude Swanson. You are absolutely right. I do not think the effort to create a General Staff will get anywhere. I am watching the situation out of the corner of my eye.

I have had a grand ten days at Hyde Park—lots of fresh air and work among my tree plantations and road building.

Love to you all,

Affectionately,
FRANKLIN D. ROOSEVELT

[Daniels had written Swanson of his fears that the Navy was trying to create a "Navy General Staff." Daniels opposed this on the grounds that it would weaken civilian control of the Navy.]

MEXICO, January 18, 1938

DEAR FRANKLIN:

I was glad to get your note some days ago and to know at first hand that you are in fine fettle.

As a constructive iconoclast, I am happy to see you breaking archaic precedents, the latest being the selection of an Irish Catholic as Ambassador to Great Britain. I never feel like applauding you so much as when you overturn an archaic or bad precedent. The older I grow the more militantly radical I become. The selection of Mr. Kennedy comes at the time when President de Valera is seeking to induce Chamberlain to recognize that all the territory of Ireland be included in the Irish Free State. Of course Mr. Kennedy will take no part in that purely domestic question, but I can well understand that like all Irishmen he would like to see Ireland free....

Affectionately yours,

JOSEPHUS DANIELS

[Joseph P. Kennedy, a Roman Catholic, was Ambassador to Great Britain from 1937 to 1941. Eamon de Valera was President of Ireland. Neville Chamberlain was the British Prime Minister.]

MEXICO, January 25, 1938

DEAR FRANKLIN:

I am enclosing you a copy of a letter I am writing to Cordell Hull today, making inquiry as to the duty of a diplomat in regard to a new service requested of an Ambassador. As you are not as staunch a prohibitionist (if propinquity makes the difference) as Cordell or myself, he may be asking your advice before making an official ruling. Should Milwaukee citizens continue to drink the stuff that made Milwaukee famous, or should I encourage the use of ardent spirits by importing the recipe for a Mexican beverage?

If neither you nor Cordell feel capable of an answer, please ring for Solomon. I await instructions.

Respectfully,
JOSEPHUS DANIELS

[Daniels had received a letter from Milwaukee asking him how to make certain Mexican cocktails and whether the ingredients could be bought in Milwaukee.]

WASHINGTON, February 1, 1938

DEAR CHIEF:

You have raised a nice question for the career men in the State Department to answer. How could you expect mere politicians like Cordell and myself to prepare a reply?

However, if I were in your place I would tell your Milwaukee friend, first, that if Milwaukee is to maintain its national reputation, it should stick to beer and not go in for hard liquor. Secondly, that you would get him the information about those Mexican drinks if you could but that not claiming to be an expert on cocktails you might send him the wrong directions and that this would be a disgrace you do not want to subject the Embassy to. A third undiplomatic reply might work equally well: "Come to Mexico and try the dirty stuff yourself."

As ever yours,
F.D.R.

WASHINGTON, March 22, 1938

DEAR CHIEF:

That is a grand story of Andre Tardieu except the part about the "kind old man." Thank the Lord neither you nor I will ever be "old men" and as long as you and I are sure of it that fact will be true.

I had to take it on the chin at an early age. The year after Eleanor and I were married, she being twenty-one and I twenty-four, we were at Campobello and had living with us her brother, Hall Roosevelt, aged sixteen. He was rather devoted to a young lady of fourteen who lived in a cottage across the way. One night he came home about 9 P.M. sighing deeply, and turning to Eleanor and me said: "Tell me something—was it customary to hold hands on the porch when you and Eleanor were young?"

As ever yours,

FRANKLIN D. ROOSEVELT

[Tardieu had written an article about the help he had in 1918 in obtaining a food allocation for France from a "kind old man" in Washington, who was Daniels.]

WASHINGTON, April 21, 1938

MY DEAR FRIENDS:

I am delighted because you are coming back to the old home in Raleigh to celebrate your Golden Wedding. What memories the anniversary will awaken in your minds and hearts— memories of joys and sorrows, of gray days and gold, through full fifty years.

Eleanor and I want you to know that with all our hearts we enter into the joy that will be yours, and none could know better than we what true happiness has been given to you. We remember your great kindness to us when we were new in Washington and an official relationship ripened into a friendship which has been among the blessings of our lives. We loved you then—we love you now—we shall love you always.

And so we join with your children and your children's children and the legion of other friends in our tribute of love and affection. May God bless you and keep you.

Very sincerely yours,
Franklin D. Roosevelt

Mexico, November 5, 1938

Telegram to Roosevelt

We heard your speech perfectly and uttered a bravo every time you knocked the opposition out of the box. You never made a greater political speech or scored as perfectly. You did well then but at thirty-six you could not measure up to the perfection of tonight's argument. My wife joins in love and congratulations.

Josephus Daniels

[On November 4, Roosevelt spoke to the nation to urge the election of liberals to state and congressional offices. "The fight for social justice and economic democracy is a long, weary uphill struggle," he said. F.D.R. specifically endorsed Herbert H. Lehman, seeking re-election as Governor of New York, and Robert F. Wagner and James M. Mead, the Democratic senatorial nominees.]

Hyde Park, November 8, 1938

Dear Chief:

Please accept my heartiest thanks for your very thoughtful telegram. I am delighted to know that you thought the speech was timely.

Kindest regards and best wishes to you and Mrs. Daniels.

As ever,

FDR

We await the polls. We may lose in a good many States—but we have some very weak candidates!

[Roosevelt's guess was sound. The Democrats suffered their first important losses since the victory of 1932. Most of the Democrats whom Roosevelt tried to purge were victorious.]

MEXICO, November 9, 1938

DEAR FRANKLIN:

You and I have not always been able to take satisfaction in election returns—in fact, in most elections we have seen our candidates defeated. All the same, the returns on Tuesday night were unexpected and depressing. The particular bright spot was New York, where we won because of your great argument and because our candidate ran on the New Deal accomplishments. Nothing delighted me more than your high praise of Wagner, and commendation of Mead. Their election gives assurance that the Empire State will ring true in the Senate, where we most need men of courage with the forward look. I was almost as glad at the defeat of O'Connor, and very happy at Lehman's election. The defeat that distressed me most was Frank Murphy in Michigan.

Among the strong influences which contributed to Republican gains, we must reckon the attitude of reactionary Democratic Senators during the last two sessions of Congress. They sowed the seed for the harvests which the Republicans reaped, some of them going down themselves because their votes and speeches gave aid and comfort to the Republican

Party. Those Senators not only hurt the party, but they themselves committed suicide.

In every reverse the Democrats have sustained in the years we have kept track of politics, the cause can largely be traced to Senators elected as Democrats who "out-Republicanized" the Republicans in their reactionary and anti-administration attitude. History repeats itself. . . .

Following Tuesday's election, we may expect the reactionary Senators to start a movement "Back to Conservatism" with another John Davis as the 1940 nominee. Our only right to live as a party and to ask for suffrage is with a liberal platform and a continuation of humane policies. If we about-face because of a few reverses, we are headed for another stay in the wilderness.

With my affectionate regards, believe me

Faithfully yours,
JOSEPHUS DANIELS

[Robert F. Wagner was Senator from New York from 1927 to 1949. Wagner won a re-election campaign in 1938 at the same time that James M. Mead, formerly a Representative, won election to the Senate for the first time. Wagner and Mead were vigorous supporters of the New Deal. Herbert H. Lehman was re-elected Governor of New York in 1938. He had been Lieutenant Governor when Roosevelt was Governor and had succeeded him in the State House at Albany. Representative John J. O'Connor of New York was the victim of Roosevelt's "purge" campaign against Conservative Democrats in 1938. Frank Murphy was elected Governor of Michigan in 1936 and was defeated for re-election in 1938. He later was appointed by Roosevelt as Attorney General and finally as a Justice of the Supreme Court. John W. Davis was the Democratic presidential nominee in 1924.]

WASHINGTON, November 14, 1938

DEAR CHIEF:

Many thanks for your notes. I am not only wholly recon-
ciled to last Tuesday's results, but I believe that they are on
the whole helpful. We have eliminated certain individuals
and certain intra-party fights which were doing positive
harm.

Curley in Massachusetts is, I hope, finally out of the picture. Quinn and O'Hara in Rhode Island tried to murder
each other and both are dead! Cross was too old a story
in Connecticut and Lonergan was a reactionary. Hague was
slapped down in New Jersey and the Pennsylvania row
brought inevitable defeat. In Ohio, Davey, the worst of our
Governors, wrecked the whole ticket.

Besides cleaning out some bad local situations, we have
on the positive side eliminated Phil LaFollette and the Farmer-
Labor people in the Northwest as a standing Third Party
threat. They must and will come to us *if* we remain definitely
the liberal party.

Frankly, I think we will have less trouble with the next
Congress than with the last. I think the idea is slowly getting
through the heads of people like Tydings and George and
Bennett Clark that even if they control the 1940 Convention
they cannot elect their ticket without the support of this
Administration—and I am sufficiently honest to decline to
support any conservative Democrat.

I am working at the present time on two very important
things—first, national defense, especially mass production of
planes; and, second, the establishment of a better system of
constant publicity with the idea not only of making clear

our objectives and methods, but also nailing the deliberate misstatements of fact as fast as they are made.

Affectionately,

FRANKLIN D. ROOSEVELT

[In this letter Roosevelt was more hopeful than the facts justified. He was trying to see the brighter side of an election that brought on an ever widening breach between Congress and the White House. His attempts to rid the Democratic Party of conservative representatives was largely unsuccessful. Roosevelt's hope that Curley is "finally out of the picture" did not come true. James M. Curley had been Democratic Mayor of Boston and Governor of Massachusetts. Despite his defeat in 1938, he was to stage a remarkable comeback, serve in the House of Representatives, a term in a federal penitentiary and again as Mayor of Boston. Augustine Lonergan was defeated in his attempt to be re-elected Senator from Connecticut. Robert E. Quinn was Governor of Rhode Island from 1937 to 1939. Walter E. O'Hara was publisher of the Providence *Star-Tribune*, which feuded with Quinn. Wilbur L. Cross was Democratic Governor of Connecticut from 1931 to 1939. Frank Hague was Mayor of Jersey City and Democratic boss of New Jersey. Martin L. Davey was Democratic Governor of Ohio from 1935 to 1939 and a critic of the New Deal. Philip F. La Follette, a Wisconsin Progressive, was Governor of his state from 1931 to 1933 and from 1935 to 1939. Senators Millard F. Tydings of Maryland, Walter F. George of Georgia, and Bennett C. Clark of Missouri were Democratic critics of Roosevelt, all re-elected in 1938 despite Roosevelt's opposition in the primaries.]

MEXICO, December 15, 1938

DEAR FRANKLIN:

I have been laboring under adverse criticism for twenty years, and I suddenly find that it ought to have been directed at you, not at me!

I recall very well that in May 1913, after the report of the General Board had been approved by Admiral Dewey, an order was issued changing "port" and "starboard" to "left" and "right." The papers tanned me thoroughly, asking what a country editor knew about the rules governing the movements of the rudder.

A few days ago I wrote to Admiral Leahy and asked him to send me a copy of the order which I thought I had signed. He has sent it to me—and lo and behold!, I find that while I clearly remember approving the report, the order which brought down the wrath of so many journalists and columnists and cartoonists upon me was signed, not by me at all, but by Franklin D. Roosevelt, Acting Secretary of the Navy.

I hereby transfer to you all the criticism which was heaped upon my head, and enclose a copy of the report and of the order—not that you will have the time to look at them now, but thinking you might wish to put them both in your files.

I expect to be in Washington shortly before Christmas and look forward to seeing you then. My wife joins me in affectionate regards to you and Eleanor.

Sincerely yours,

JOSEPHUS DANIELS

[Fleet Admiral William D. Leahy was Chief of Staff to Roosevelt in World War II. He was Chief of Naval Operations from 1937 to 1939.]

The following are pencilled notes by Daniels dated January 14, 1939:

"We had dinner at the White House last night and I made an engagement to see the President (U.S.) next morning. Sumner Welles told me that FDR had agreed to see Patrick Hurley (Oil company attorney) who had gone to Mexico to talk oil settlement, and he (Welles) thought it would be a good idea if I was present when Hurley made his report. I repeated that to the President and he thought it best. I also gave him my strong view that the expropriation was chiefly due to the color difficulty and could have been averted if the companies had been willing to pay fair wages, & that I believed he ought to decline to touch the matter until the oil companies had shown a willingness to negotiate with the Mexican Govt. I also told him that they had even refused to cooperate in an inventory at the time of expropriation....

"In a long talk at the White House with President Roosevelt today he told me that an intercepted German order addressed to Ambassador Ribbentrop contained specific plans for an air-raid attack by Germans on London before the Munich meeting. Germany and Italy had 13,000 effective combat planes. Together Britain & France had only 1,900 that were ready. The German plan was to begin the attack at 11 o'clock at night with 100 planes and send 100 additional ones every hour to bomb London. The British said they had power to ward off the first 2 or 3 attacks, but their munitions and resources could not resist after the first 500 German bombing planes. This knowledge made Chamberlain capitulate at Munich. FDR also said that there was nothing to the talk that the Germans were undernourished, to the contrary the trained German fighting men were strong and in the pink of condition. I did not ask FDR from whom he obtained this information which he accepted as accurate, but as he had recently talked with Ambassadors Kennedy of Britain, Bullitt of France and Wilson from Germany I am quite sure that was the source of the information which had evidently been fully verified by him. When I expressed some doubt as to the great superiority of the totalitarian countries, he said he was so convinced of its accuracy that if he had been in Chamberlain's place he would have felt constrained to have made terms to prevent the war for which Germany was fully prepared. He remarked he could not understand how Britain and France could have permitted themselves to get in such comparative weak positions.

"Referring to a recent visit from Lord (I didn't catch his name) the President said the Lord had told him that if Anglo-Saxon leadership was to be preserved in the world it was up to the United States to do the job, that Britain was through. He related to FDR that in former times when the British representative in Egypt wished a certain course pursued, he would send for the ranking Egyptian official to come to see him, and tell him what to do. Now the Briton goes to see the Egyptian. . . .

"FDR, speaking of our obligations under the Monroe Doctrine, indicated that the first danger to us would come from Brazil. I asked if it was because there were nearly a million Germans in Brazil; he answered, 'There are a million and a half. When ready to send armadas of bombing planes from Africa (look how Africa juts out on the map) is ready to fly to Brazil [sic] a civil war would be started there and German planes will swoop down from Africa on Brazil to decide the war in favor [of] Germany.' He spoke as if that might be the real danger to this continent.

"Adverting to the recent visit of Anthony Eden, I said I had found many Americans who pinned their faith in Eden. He didn't share their faith and said that in the two conversations he had with Eden he was not impressed with his capacity for leadership. He undoubtedly has ability but not greatness or the qualities for successful leadership.

"Going from the White House, I found Secretary Hull in a more pessimistic mood about Pan America than I had expected after his public report of the Lima Conference. He thinks Germany is trying to get footholds there by barter transactions and otherwise."

[Sumner Welles was Under Secretary of State. Patrick J. Hurley was former Secretary of War. Joseph P. Kennedy was Ambassador to Great Britain, William C. Bullitt Ambassador to France and Hugh R. Wilson to Germany. Anthony Eden was British Foreign Secretary. Joachim von Ribbentrop was German Ambassador to Great Britain.]

On April 14, 1939, Daniels recorded these notes following a meeting with the President:

"On the occasion of my visit to the White House, after the dinner the President turning to my wife, said: 'The Chief and I will have a talk in the library while you and Mrs. R. and the others chat in Mrs. R's room.' We talked—or rather he talked—for nearly an hour about legislation and the political future. He said that as to legislation, that the so-called conservatives would be given the opportunity to take responsibility. He would recommend what he thought was needed and leave it to them to cut so deep that people would go hungry or be denied work which was needed.

"As to politics, FDR said that he did not believe the Democratic party would avert defeat by repudiating the New Deal policies—that the nomination of a reactionary would invite and receive a crushing defeat—and that he would not feel called upon to take any part in a campaign of repudiation of liberal and progressive policies. . . .

"He talked about internal administration—did not think the War Department was functioning as well as it should. He intimated that changes would be made. I look to see Frank Murphy succeed as Secretary of War after a brief term in the Senate and Robert Jackson made Attorney General. FDR did not mention Jackson, but did indicate that Murphy would go to War. He was a soldier and made a fine record in the Philippines. After FDR had talked of this, I asked: 'What about the Navy?' He said that Claude Swanson was too sick a man to do much 'but I haven't the heart to let him go. He depends on his salary for a living and I just couldn't ask him to quit.'. . . He talked more about the Navy, and, continuing again about Swanson's health, said with a sort of smile, 'You know I am my own Secretary of the Navy.' Of course I knew that and told him that I remarked to my wife when he was inaugurated that, whatever else went on in the administration, FDR would really be Secretary of the Navy, and I said, 'You just couldn't help it.' He chuckled."

[Frank Murphy, who was Attorney General, was nominated a Justice of the Supreme Court in January, 1940. He never served in the Senate. Robert H. Jackson succeeded

Murphy as Attorney General and the next year was appointed to the Supreme Court. Swanson died on July 7, 1939.]

WASHINGTON, February 15, 1939

DEAR CHIEF:

I am somewhat concerned because the people with whom I have recently been talking regarding the Mexican oil question tell me that the impression exists in Mexico that I have condoned "seizure without just compensation" of American-owned oil properties by the Mexican Government.

I wish you would see President Cardenas at as early a date as may be possible and make very clear to him two things:

First, of course, I fully recognize the right of every sovereign government such as Mexico to expropriate property under its jurisdiction. It is, however, the long-established rule of international law, as well as one of the most necessary principles in healthy international relationships, that when a government finds it necessary to expropriate, expropriation be accompanied by fair compensation. That is the position that I myself have maintained in relation to property taken by this Government for flood control and power and navigation purposes during the past six years and I have been consistent in maintaining the same position with regard to the expropriation by Mexico of these American-owned oil properties. I have in no way and at no time condoned expropriation by Mexico without at the same time offering just compensation.

Second, Donald Richberg is taking with him to Mexico as a basis for negotiation with the Mexican Government a proposal which seems to me eminently practical. The proposal will make it possible for the companies to recoup the value of the properties over a period of years through a reasonable share of the profits obtained under a management contract, and will at the same time make it possible for the companies yearly to pay cash on the barrelhead to the Mexican Government in the form of a franchise tax—or whatever it may be decided to call it—which tax will vary in amount depending upon the total profits made. As I understand it, when the contract is terminated, the companies have nothing further to do with the properties. Thus, there is, as I see it, a tacit recognition of the right of the Mexican Government to expropriate without any further ado. The mere fact of the contract itself and of the payment of a franchise tax on a sliding scale, plus termination of any interest on the part of the companies at the end of the contract not only saves everybody's face but also brings cold cash to the Mexican Government. That is much to be desired. I wish you would do your utmost to impress upon President Cardenas that I believe this proposal offers a fair basis for agreement and that I consider it of the utmost importance in the interest of the two countries that an agreement be found at a very early moment.

My best regards to you both, and believe me

Affectionately yours,

FRANKLIN D. ROOSEVELT

[Donald R. Richberg was an attorney for the oil companies who went to Mexico in an unsuccessful attempt to settle the controversy over Mexico's oil expropriation act of 1938.]

MEXICO, July 7, 1939

DEAR FRANKLIN:

If you have no other plans I would deem it a great honor

to be named as Secretary of the Navy to succeed our friend Claude Swanson.

My past experience would enable me to press to completion your big navy program and assist you in furthering the large program for the public weal that lies ahead of you. My health was never so good as now.

With my affectionate regards,

JOSEPHUS DANIELS

This amazing request by Daniels, when he already was seventy-seven years old, at least shows how he felt about himself and Father Time. Daniels was in excellent health; he felt a certain proprietary interest in F.D.R.; he loved the Navy, and since 1933 he had wanted to be closer than Mexico City was to the scene of action. Despite his years, he was young in spirit and outlook. He talked about being a young man and in many ways he was.

Two years later, at the age of seventy-nine, when he resigned as Ambassador because of his wife's health, Daniels stopped in Washington to see his son, Dr. Worth B. Daniels, a distinguished physician. To a friend who thought Daniels might be going to see his son or one of his associates for a physical check-up, the retiring Ambassador said: "I am going to see Worth to talk about my future." He said it as matter-of-factly as a young man just out of college.

At seventy-nine, Daniels returned to Raleigh to become editor again of his *News and Observer*. He continued at that active task until his death in 1948, just before his eighty-sixth birthday.

Despite the importance of the letter of July 7 to Roosevelt (a pencilled copy is in the Daniels papers at the Library of Congress and the original is in the Franklin D. Roosevelt

Library at Hyde Park) there is no evidence that F.D.R. replied to it. Instead of naming Daniels, he promoted Charles Edison, son of Thomas A. Edison, from the assistant secretaryship.

MEXICO, September 12, 1939

DEAR FRANKLIN:

Mr. Welles forwarded me your letter to President Cardenas and requested me to deliver it in person. By appointment I called on Friday and discussed with him the important suggestions which you made, to-wit, that all the matters of difference pending between the two governments, some of long standing, should be adjusted, so that all the problems operating to disturb the harmonious relations be removed. He bade me to tell you that he earnestly desires the attainment of the goal you propose and will be glad to cooperate to that end. He said he would read your letter and all of the proposals it contains will receive his friendly consideration. He added that he would like to see me again. In Mexican parlance, I told him, "I am at your orders."

President Cardenas discussed at length the situation that had been produced by the war, saying that no country could be indifferent because it affected every country, no matter how remote from the seat of war. He instanced that it had already adversely affected railroad construction in the southern part of Mexico. His country had ordered rails from Germany (paying for these in oil and I think in advance of delivery) but that shipment was held up by the war. The consequence is that railroad construction is retarded and men employed in such work are now out of their jobs.

President Cardenas said he was in sincere sympathy with the purpose of the Panama Conference to be held on the

21st and thought continental solidarity was essential to every nation on this hemisphere. His country will be represented by General Eduardo Hay, the Minister of Foreign Relations.

I trust that Congress, while holding firmly for the neutrality of our country, will follow your suggestions. I am 100 per cent against out participation in this criminal war, but, of course, I trust that Europe will be delivered from totalitarian governments and the scourge of Force. This hemisphere must be vaccinated against the European war miasma.

With my affectionate regards,

Faithfully yours,

JOSEPHUS DANIELS

[The second World War broke out in Europe on September 1. As in the early days of World War I, Daniels wanted the United States to remain neutral. However, in 1939-40, he was much more aware of the necessity for an allied victory than he had been in 1914-15.]

MEXICO, November 4, 1939

DEAR FRANKLIN:

When I returned from Washington I requested the Foreign Minister to arrange for me to see President Cardenas when it was convenient. He was in his home State, Michoacan, and did not return until recently. Yesterday, November 3rd, I called on him by appointment at the Palace, and delivered your message of sincere regards and your earnest hope for a meeting with him when you could face to face discuss the mutual aims and problems of the two neighbor republics. General Cardenas appeared gratified at your cordial message which I delivered in the friendly spirit with which you imparted it to me. He replied that he fully reciprocated your desire for a personal meeting and exchange of views and that he would arrange his time to suit a date and place most agreeable to you. I hope you will come to this city when you are able to arrange the time.

President Cardenas said that he felt encouraged with regard to the petroleum negotiations. He said that he had replied to your cordial letter on the subject, indicating that the Mexican Government was entirely in accord with the idea of a comprehensive settlement of problems between the two countries. He said that Ambassador Castillo Najera had seen you on his return to Washington and had conveyed to you his reply; that you had made some useful comments and it now looked as though Mr. Richberg might come back soon to Mexico to discuss matters further on the bases indicated by you. President Cardenas said that he felt that progress had been made in the petroleum matter and that in the next two months the matter might find solution....

Faithfully yours,

JOSEPHUS DANIELS

MEXICO, November 6, 1939

DEAR ELEANOR AND FRANKLIN (You see I am putting first
    things first):

My bookshelves are enriched by many Roosevelt books and Roosevelt documents and addresses. I feel that there ought to be some reciprocity, even though you get the short end. Therefore, and because of my affection, I have requested the publishers to send you a copy of my book *Tar Heel Editor* which I have autographed. It deals entirely with my life in North Carolina up to 1893 when I went to Washington as Chief Clerk of the Interior Department under Cleveland

and had a small part in the beginnings of the creation of the State of Oklahoma.

If the book has any interest it is because I have told the story, with actual names of people, of a small Southern town in the late seventies and middle eighties and of men and movements that as an editor I observed—"these things I saw and part of them I was"—from 1885 to 1893 in the capital of North Carolina. I do not flatter myself that outside North Carolina the book will have much demand, even if there, but I felt impelled to write it for my own satisfaction.

The second volume will deal with the second Cleveland Administration, the Cleveland-Bryan party duel and North Carolina politics up to 1912, when our paths come together until 1921. Most of this I wrote before coming here. The third volume (some of which I wrote shortly after leaving Washington in 1921) will deal with men and events from 1921 to 1932. I plan a last volume dealing with the era from 1933, the New Deal and Mexico, but I will write none of it until I lay down public office....

With my affectionate regards,

Faithfully yours,

JOSEPHUS DANIELS

[Daniels was a prolific writer all his life. He wrote editorials, columns, magazine articles, and books. His books are *Life of Worth Bagley* (1898), *The Navy and the Nation* (1919), *Our Navy at War* (1922) and *The Life of Woodrow Wilson* (1924). *Tar Heel Editor* (1939) was the first of a five-volume autobiography. The other volumes are *Editor in Politics* (1940), *The Wilson Era, Years of Peace* (1944), *The Wilson Era, Years of War and After* (1945), and *Shirt-Sleeve Diplomat* (1947).]

MEXICO, Jan. 29, 1940

DEAR FRANKLIN:

My wife joins in sending love and birthday good wishes. It must warm your heart that your countrymen celebrate this day in carrying out humanitarian benefactions which you inspired.

I wish we were near enough to call on your birthday and exchange views upon matters in which we have a common interest. As distance prevents we send you our felicitations and hope to be present when you celebrate your one hundredth anniversary.

Love to Mrs. Roosevelt.

Faithfully,

JOSEPHUS DANIELS

WASHINGTON, February 1, 1940

DEAR CHIEF:

Ever so many thanks for that delightful birthday note. I hope to get away for a little holiday in a couple of weeks— the first since my interrupted vacation last August and I am taking with me your very wonderful book.

I am part way through it and I want to tell you that I consider it one of the greatest contributions to recent history that I have ever read and you have handled the whole subject to perfection. Several other people have told me that they, too, consider it a masterpiece, combining fact with charm of presentation. All I can say is, I hope you are working hard on the next volume.

We have been having a very cold winter for Washington and almost everybody has had, or is about to come down with, a mild form of "flu." I envy you.

Affectionately yours,

FRANKLIN D. ROOSEVELT

HYDE PARK, May 6, 1940

DEAR CHIEF:

My hearty congratulations on the three milestones which meet in such happy conjunction: the seventy-eighth anniversary of your birth, the seventy-fifth anniversary of the establishment of the *News and Observer*, and the forty-sixth of your ownership of that outstanding newspaper.

It is by a fortunate coincidence that these three anniversaries are to be commemorated in a Diamond Jubilee Edition of the paper which has been for so long under your ownership and able direction.

During a long life of varied activity and singular usefulness you have been called many times from your newspaper to serve the public in high posts of great responsibility. As Secretary of the Navy you discharged the duties of a difficult position with vision and resourcefulness during a period of grave emergency. As Ambassador to Mexico, you have devoted superb talents in tact and diplomacy to strengthening the policy of the good neighbor in international relations.

In whatever field you have been called to serve you have been a powerful advocate and earnest exemplar of true Americanism. We think of you first of all as an editor who has been a preeminent leader in the formulation of public opinion in the affairs of the great State of North Carolina and of the Nation. Despite the many honors which have come to you outside the field of your chosen profession, I feel that none has been more welcome than the acclaim which has come to you as a newspaper man who through more than two score years has been unwearied in upholding the highest ideals of American journalism.

Mrs. Roosevelt joins me in this greeting and in the heartfelt wish that you may be spared for long years to come to continue your labors in behalf of peace and good will among men and nations.

With oldtime regard and affection,

> Very sincerely yours,
>
> FRANKLIN D. ROOSEVELT

Daniels took a brief home leave in May, 1940, so that he and Mrs. Daniels could celebrate the triple anniversary in Raleigh. But with the world seemingly falling apart, Daniels was restless to be in harness, and he still wanted a more active role than his assignment to Mexico. He felt very deeply the tragedy of the Second World War.

> RALEIGH, May 22, 1940

DEAR FRANKLIN:

When I know the strain under which you and your associates are laboring, I feel almost like a slacker to be taking leave. I have written Cordell I am ready to fly back to Mexico any day, and I am writing to tell you what you already know, that I am "at your orders" (that's a favorite expression in Mexico) ready to go anywhere or do anything at any time in these terrible days. Little did we think in 1919 that another holocaust would come in our day. I pray that you may have guidance.

> Affectionately,
>
> JOSEPHUS DANIELS

P.S. I suppose you read that the North Carolina delegation to Chicago were instructed unanimously to vote for your nomination. I am a delegate-at-large and expect to fly up from Mexico to Chicago.

Neither of the North Carolina senators is on the delegation to the Chicago Convention.   JD

[The North Carolina Senators in 1940 were Josiah W. Bailey and Robert R. Reynolds—both anti-Roosevelt.]

WASHINGTON, May 25, 1940

DEAR CHIEF:

I have your letter and you know how much I appreciate your words of encouragement. I shall keep your offer of service always in mind, but you are "at it" now—splendidly.

With best wishes,

Very sincerely yours,
FRANKLIN D. ROOSEVELT

WASHINGTON, June 12, 1940

DEAR CHIEF:

You and Mrs. Daniels were angels to send me that grand Indian bed cover. Thank you ever so much. It is going to Hyde Park with me for the new cottage the next time I go up. When that will be, I have no idea. As you know, I have been trying for weeks now to get up there for a week end but have not felt that I could go that far away, even for a short time.

My affectionate regards to you and Mrs. Daniels.

As ever,
F.D.R.

MEXICO, September 19, 1940

DEAR FRANKLIN:

...I do not suppose you were surprised at the open advocacy of Willkie by the *New York Times*, for it has never sounded a truly liberal note.... In many ways it is a great newspaper and it is a thousand pities that in measures that look to the welfare of the masses it has no heart.

In this connection I recall what President Wilson said toward the close of his administration when the *Times* was celebrating an important anniversary and was preparing to print congratulations from distinguished men all over the world. Mr. Wiley asked me to request President Wilson to write such a letter. In view of the *Times'* support of the administration's policy during the war and the League of Nations, I undertook to persuade Mr. Wilson to write a congratulatory letter. He not only refused, but said: "I am tired of being urged to send congratulations that would be construed as approval of that paper. Its managers have asked Grayson and others to request such a commendation. I declined. They still persist. I hate not to comply with your request, but I will not write a letter of commendation for a paper which has never had a word of approval of the social and economic reforms for which the Administration has stood." He said this, or the substance of it, with evident warmth... As a journalist I am troubled that most prosperous big papers become Big Business and no longer speak out for the reforms that are necessary for the need of the many....

Affectionately,

JOSEPHUS DANIELS

[The *New York Times*, an independent Democratic newspaper, supported Roosevelt in 1932, 1936, and 1944. In 1940 it endorsed Wendell L. Willkie, the Republican candidate. Louis Wiley was business manager of the *Times*. Rear Admiral Cary T. Grayson was President Wilson's physician.]

WASHINGTON, September 28, 1940

DEAR CHIEF:

Thank you for that very illuminating letter about, among other things, the *New York Times*. I know you will not mind if I say to you that the more I see of American newspapers the more I am convinced that they represent, in nine cases out of ten, the personal slant or point of view not of the publisher, not of the editor, not of the public, not even of the advertiser, but of the fellow who owns the paper!

The second observation I have to make is that when the owner reaches a certain position of affluence—in other words, gets into the higher brackets of the personal income tax, he begins to associate with other Americans in the same rarefied upper brackets. He decreases his association with the little fellow, he begins to believe that the Hamiltonian theory was correct—and especially he and his family thrill over their membership in social circles. Soon the check book and the securities market supplant the old patriotism and the old desire to purvey straight news to the public.

Thank God that you and the boys prove that though it is an exceptional case, ownership can still retain the old ideals of editorship.

About fifteen years ago I attended one of the famous luncheons in the French mahogany carved sanctum of the *New York Times*. In that rarefied atmosphere of self-anointed scholars, I had the feeling of an uneducated worm under the microscope. But, the America of the satisfied professors will not survive, and the America of *you* and of *me* will.

As ever yours,

FRANKLIN D. ROOSEVELT

MEXICO, November 6, 1940

TELEGRAM TO ROOSEVELT

Felicitations and congratulations and love. I am sure you will be governed by the immortal admonition in the eighth verse of the sixth chapter of Micah.

JOSEPHUS DANIELS

[Roosevelt was elected for a third term on November 5, 1940, defeating Willkie but not by so large a majority as he had defeated Hoover and Landon.]

WASHINGTON, November 8, 1940

DEAR CHIEF:

Thank you for your message of congratulation and affection. The reference to Micah is timely, for the sum of all of our duties and obligations is found in the admonition: "to do justly, to love mercy, and to walk humbly with thy God."

Eleanor joins me in love to you and Mrs. Daniels.

Very sincerely yours,

FRANKLIN D. ROOSEVELT

WASHINGTON, January 2, 1941

DEAR CHIEF:

I am thrilled to have *Editor in Politics*—it is one of my most prized Christmas gifts. Ever so many thanks.

This carries to you and Mrs. Daniels my very affectionate

greetings for the New Year. I look forward to seeing you before you return to Mexico.

> Affectionately,
> FRANKLIN D. ROOSEVELT

WASHINGTON, February 14, 1941

DEAR CHIEF:

I did read your perfectly grand speech at the Electoral College Banquet, and I am particularly glad that you brought out that old effort of mine to get into the war—when I was only thirty-five years old.

Do you remember the other and final chapter? When I had nearly finished the inspection work on the other side in September, 1918, I think I wrote you or cabled that after I had come home and reported to you, I wanted to go back to Europe with an assignment, in uniform, to the Naval Railway Battery. Good old Admiral Plunkett had talked with me about it at St. Nazaire in France where the guns were being assembled and were nearly ready. He asked me if I could swear well enough in French to swear a French train on to a siding and let his big guns through. Thereupon, with certain inventive genius, I handed him a line of French swear words, real and imaginary, which impressed him greatly and he said that he would take me on, if I came back, in his outfit with the rank of lieutenant commander.

A little later, as you remember, I came back on the Leviathan with "flu" and a touch of pneumonia and was laid up in New York and Hyde Park for about three weeks. I got back to the Department, as I remember it, about the twentieth of October, told you of my desire, and you said that you could not conscientiously ask me to stay in Washington any longer. Then I went to see the President and the President told me that in his judgment I was too late—that he had received the first suggestions of an armistice from Prince Max of Baden, and that he hoped the war would be over very soon.

That ended the effort on my part because within a few days it was clear that some form of armistice would be worked out.

Love to you both,

Affectionately,

FRANKLIN D. ROOSEVELT

[Rear Admiral Charles P. Plunkett commanded the 14-inch naval railway batteries in France in 1918.]

MEXICO, March 11, 1941

DEAR FRANKLIN:

Shortly after my return, as I wrote you, I called to see President Avila Camacho and conveyed your belief that the good of both countries required enlarged naval and air bases for the protection of this hemisphere in case of attack. I added that you wished nothing done that would give any other country control or ownership of a foot of Mexican soil—all you wished was to be helpful in the Mexican desire to construct such bases so that they would be available co-operatively to Pan American countries in case continental solidarity might be in peril....

Do not let the hectic stories about Nazi agents and Fifth Columnists worry you. There are such creatures here but our own and Mexicans are vigilant and diligent and they will not be permitted to do much.

My wife joins in affectionate regards to you and Eleanor. You are much in our thoughts in these grave days and sometimes I wish that I could help you more.

Affectionately,

JOSEPHUS DANIELS

ON BOARD U.S.S. *Potomac*, March 28, 1941

DEAR CHIEF:

I have read with much interest your letter of March 11, 1941 regarding various Mexican matters and particularly the question of cooperation between the United States and Mexico in continental defense. I entirely agree with your decision to refrain for the present from discussing the question of financing by the United States of Mexican defense construction works. If and when the necessity arises for financial assistance on our part, I shall have the situation explored promptly.

We have all been greatly encouraged by the friendly and cooperative attitude of the Mexican Government and of the Mexican Foreign Minister in particular in these matters of mutual interest. It does seem that Mexico realizes the sincerity of the United States in its Good Neighbor policy and is preparing to go as far as necessary with us along the paths of friendship and collaboration.

I read with deep interest the enclosures to your letter, copies of reports you had sent to the Department of State.

My affectionate regards to you both.

Very sincerely yours,

FRANKLIN D. ROOSEVELT

WASHINGTON, April 1, 1941

DEAR CHIEF:

I had really hoped that I could carry out the plan of meeting President Camacho in Mexican waters this March or April.

I hope you will tell him this and also that my only reason is that I felt that at this time I ought to be within twenty-four hours of Washington in view of the rapidity with which things are happening. Actually and confidentially, my little trip on the U.S.S. *Potomac* took me to the northern and western Bahamas, not more than four hours from the Florida railroad at any time.

Personally, as you know, I would love to make arrangements by which I could fly back from the Tampico or Veracruz coast in case of emergency—but everybody is very definitely set against my using the air.

Tell the President that the same thing applies to Warm Springs where I may go for a week after Easter but, as you know, I can get back to Washington from there in about eighteen hours.

Therefore, I have to keep the whole thing open until such time as the Balkan problems quiet down and the shipping problem becomes at least no worse. I am most anxious to meet President Camacho and I know that he and I would be in every way simpatico. . . .

As ever yours,
FRANKLIN D. ROOSEVELT

[The Balkan problem was the impending German attack on Yugoslavia. The shipping problem was the high rate of sinkings by Nazi U-boats.]

HYDE PARK, May 31, 1941

DEAR CHIEF:

I meant to send you a line on your birthday. You are dead right when you say that you feel young and act young. Most certainly you and I have got to celebrate your hundredth birthday together, and I will come to Raleigh for it.

Much love to you both,

As ever yours,
FRANKLIN D. ROOSEVELT

[Daniels was seventy-nine on May 18.]

HYDE PARK, July 3, 1941

DEAR CHIEF:

I am delighted that you sent me the story about President Wilson when he was asked to find the superman. I shall use it.

Of course, we have to put up, now as then, with people who have no idea what Government as such means. Most of the wildeyed suggestions utterly fail to specify facts.

All we can do is the best we can do.

As ever yours,
FRANKLIN D. ROOSEVELT

[Daniels had written Roosevelt regarding proposals, widespread at the time, for appointing a defense "czar." Daniels recalled that Wilson faced similar demands in 1917 and that Wilson had said: "You ask me to find a man with all wisdom and entrust the preparation and conduct of the war to him. Please name the man who can measure up to that great task. . . . There is no such superman as you demand. It is a god you want and I am sorry to say I have no gods at my disposal."]

WASHINGTON, October 30, 1941

DEAR FRANKLIN:

It is with sincere regret that I am impelled by family reasons to tender my resignation as your Ambassador to Mexico, to which diplomatic post you did me the honor to appoint me in March 1933. The physicians of my wife advise that her health will not justify her continuance in the responsible though agreeable duties which devolve upon the wife of the Ambassador to Mexico. And no one knows better than you that I cannot carry on without her.

It gives us both a sense of the deepest regret to sever the delightful relations with friends in the Mexican Government, colleagues in the diplomatic corps of which I am dean, members of our Embassy staff and many Mexican and other friends with whom our associations have been so pleasant that we will ever cherish them. During our stay in Mexico we have been the recipients of the most gracious hospitality.

When you did me the honor to nominate me to the post I am now relinquishing, I went to Mexico animated by a single purpose: to incarnate your policy of the Good Neighbor. My constant aim has been to truly interpret the friendship of our country to our nearest southern neighbors. I have visited all parts of the republic as a Good Will Ambassador, never asking anything for any of my countrymen except what our country extends to Mexicans sojourning in the United States. I am glad to report to you that from the day of assuming the duties I have found cordial reciprocation of the sentiment of friendship expressed in your inaugural address.

In laying down the duties, I need not assure you of my appreciation for the opportunity of serving our country in this important post. I know also that I need not tell you of my happiness in having been a part of your administration which has been distinguished by its devotion to the common weal, and which has, in conjunction with the other twenty Pan-American republics, secured continental solidarity. I am happy to tell you that the relations between Mexico and the United States are on the most sincerely friendly basis in their history and that both are firmly united to prevent any infiltration of alien isms or forces on this hemisphere from any quarter.

In the great tasks that lie ahead, I will be happy, with voice and pen and in any other way that opens, to give any aid in carrying out the great policies for which your administration has won world approval.

Affectionately yours,
JOSEPHUS DANIELS

WASHINGTON, October 31, 1941

DEAR CHIEF:

As you know, I have been worried for some time about your wife's health and hoping all the while that it would justify you both staying on in Mexico.

Nevertheless, it comes to me as a real shock that we have to face the situation and that the country will have to do without the services of its Ambassador to Mexico, who perhaps, more than anyone else, has exemplified the true spirit of the good neighbor in the foreign field.

That you have succeeded so completely is the testimony that in a position which, as we all know, was difficult when you first assumed it, our relations with our southern neighbors have, largely because of you, become relations of understanding and real friendship.

I know that you will miss your colleagues and friends in Mexico City and I think you can realize my own feelings in not having my old Chief as an intimate part of the Administration.

However, what must be, must be. I can only hope that your good wife's health will improve in her own home in Raleigh.

I think that it is right that you should make a short trip to Mexico City in order to take farewell of all your friends there, and to present my very warm personal regards to President Camacho and to his Secretary of State for Foreign Affairs.

I hope, therefore, that it will be agreeable if I do not accept your resignation until you have returned from a short visit to Mexico and completed such leave as may be due you.

With my affectionate regards to you both, I am

As ever yours,

FRANKLIN D. ROOSEVELT

WASHINGTON, November 26, 1941

DEAR CHIEF:

Referring to your letter of October 30 and to mine of October 31 concerning your resignation as Ambassador to Mexico, I am informed by the Secretary of State that your authorized leave of absence will expire at the close of business on January 20, 1942. For the completion of the record therefore, I formally accept your resignation to be effective at the close of business on January 20, 1942—with my affectionate and deep regrets!

Very sincerely yours,

FRANKLIN D. ROOSEVELT

After ending his diplomatic career at the age of seventy-nine, Daniels returned to Raleigh to resume his editorial duties. While he was in Mexico, three of his sons ran the *News and Observer*—Frank and Josephus, Jr., were the business and advertising directors and Jonathan was editor. Shortly after Daniels returned to Raleigh, Jonathan went to Washington as Assistant Director of the Office of Civilian Defense. Later he became administrative assistant and finally press secretary to Roosevelt. Daniels continued to be in good health and gave vigorous direction to the paper, writing most of the editorials himself. His health was unimpaired until a few weeks before his death from pneumonia in 1948. Despite the fact that Daniels spent most of his life reading and writing, he never wore glasses.

WASHINGTON, May 18, 1942

TELEGRAM TO DANIELS

Hearty congratulations on reaching the fourscore mark full of fight for all good causes, with face resolutely to the future and young in everything save years. Eleanor joins me in affectionate greetings to you and Mrs. Daniels. You both become dearer to us with every passing year.

FRANKLIN D. ROOSEVELT

[Daniels was eighty years old on May 18.]

RALEIGH, May 20, 1942

DEAR FRANKLIN:

I need not tell you how much my wife and I appreciated your loving message.

You are constantly in our thoughts and in our prayers that you may have guidance and direction in these difficult hours. It must hearten you and give you strength to know of the confidence of the people and their affection.

My wife and boys join me in love to you and Eleanor and in the hope that one of these days we shall foregather as of old.

Affectionately,

JOSEPHUS DANIELS

WASHINGTON, July 30, 1942

DEAR CHIEF: .

Keep up the good work. You are going strong and accomplishing a world of good. We, of course, are going through a very difficult phase of the war—on the fighting front, and on the home front.

If these Russians will hold their armies intact until snow flies I shall feel much better, for I am convinced that 1943 will see all the United Nations in far better shape than in 1942.

On the home front we must contend against the Congress which would conduct the war 531 different ways but I am mostly concerned by these fool commentators and columnists, for they disseminate not opinions, which is their right, but false statements of fact, which is not their right.

As ever yours,

F.D.R.

RALEIGH, Oct. 3, 1942

DEAR FRANKLIN:

You are everlastingly right. Most of the pessimism is born in Washington and comes from officials who ought to be ashamed of their disloyalty, congressmen who have been dawdling all

summer and some columnists and commentators and other
calumniators . . .

Affectionately,

JOSEPHUS DANIELS

RALEIGH, November 6, 1942

DEAR FRANKLIN:

I know you are too busy to read editorials from the pro-
vincial journals, but I am enclosing two which appeared in
The News and Observer, and my article about "Stoning the
Prophets," referring to the defeat of George Norris.

I write a column in *The News and Observer* called The
Rhamkatte Roaster, a mythical paper, and which I attribute to
the "Old Codger." Neither, of course, exists but it enables me
to get some things off my chest that I wish to say. This article
on "Stoning the Prophets" is a sort of article which if written
by Louis Howe, he would call "a masterpiece."

I hope all goes well with you. With my highest regards,

Faithfully yours,

JOSEPHUS DANIELS

[The Rhamkatte Roaster was a column Daniels wrote in
which the "Old Codger" always spoke his mind freely. He
likened the defeat of Norris to the stoning of the prophets in
Jerusalem. "Out in Nebrasky," the "Old Codger" said, "sum
Democrats an' many Reypublikins, as blind as Saul wuz, jined
in the hue an' cry an' political stonin' ov George Norris."
Senator George W. Norris, the Nebraska Independent who
had been in the House and Senate for forty years, was defeated
in 1942 by Kenneth S. Wherry, a Republican.]

WASHINGTON, November 10, 1942

DEAR CHIEF:

I like those editorials a lot and I am glad you are starting "The Rhamkatte Roaster."

I am deeply distressed about poor old George Norris. He seemed to be quite sunk after his defeat.

I am happy today in the fact that for three months I have been taking it on the chin in regard to the Second Front and that this is now over. The expeditions seem to be moving well. I hate the subterfuge of communiques which use the phrase "moving according to plan," as that is often a cloak for the stalling of an operation. In the case in Africa, the phrase is, however, true—so far.

Affectionately,

FRANKLIN D. ROOSEVELT

[The first important allied offensive of World War II began on November 8, 1942, when General Eisenhower's forces landed in North Africa.]

RALEIGH, January 28, 1943

DEAR FRANKLIN:

I was never more cheered and happy in my life than at your going to Casablanca and putting life and action into the great struggle in which we are engaged. I am sure it will accelerate the offensive.

You know that my wife is the second Sherlock Holmes. Shortly after you left, and it was "norated" that you had gone away on some official visit, and when most people supposed you were making another tour to look at the American arsenal, my wife asked one day: "Where do you think Franklin has gone?" My imagination is not as good as hers. Neither is my foresight, so I asked in Yankee fashion: "Where do you think?"

She replied that you had gone to North Africa, and she was so confident that she was one of the few persons not surprised at all when it was announced.

It was a great adventure and heartened all the Democracies of the world. God bless and keep you.

Love to you and Eleanor in which my wife joins,

Affectionately,

JOSEPHUS DANIELS

[Roosevelt went to Casablanca to meet Prime Minister Churchill and other war leaders in January, 1943. The fact that the President had left the country was not announced until his safe return.]

RALEIGH, February 16, 1943

DEAR FRANKLIN:

It made me very happy to see you and I came home sharing your confidence.

My wife was very much pleased that you gave her the reputation, among the editors, of having a sixth sense....

Faithfully yours,

JOSEPHUS DANIELS

Roosevelt held a special press conference for the American Society of Newspaper Editors on February 12. Daniels was one of the editors present. Roosevelt said the first thing he wanted to do was to thank the editors for keeping secret his absence from the country to attend the Casablanca conference. He continued: "I think it was a better—better kept secret than any other one that has happened in the country for a long time. You did a grand job. Of course, you didn't all know just where I was. (laughter)

"But my old Chief's wife guessed that I was in Africa. She was about the only one that did. (more laughter) The Chief said that she had always had—Mrs. Daniels always had a sort of sixth sense on things like that. So I wrote him back to tell Mrs. Daniels that I had always known that in the old days.

"Oh, back around 1913-14, we had in the Navy a very clever and brilliant Rear Admiral by the name of Bradley Fiske....

"Well, old man Fiske, about—Oh, five or half-past, when the Secretary was thinking of going home, almost every day would bring him a long twelve- or twenty-page typewritten technical article on armor, or some new form of machine gun, or something like that, which no layman could possibly understand, and tell the Secretary he had to read that because he wanted action on it in the morning.

"And I knew what he did with them, but I wasn't always sure.

"So he went away one day. And Bradley Fiske came around to see me, and he said, 'I have got to have action on about three different documents that I left with the Secretary.'

"I said, 'Where are they?'

" 'I don't know. I can't find the documents on his desk.'

"I picked up the telephone. I called up Mrs. Daniels, and I said they were lost, and she said, 'Hmm—' —thought a minute— 'I think I can find them.'

"I think you know in those days most of the politicians wore those long, full-tailed cutaway coats.

"And she said, 'I am going up to his closet. I think they are in the right-hand rear tail of his spare cutaway coat.' (loud laughter)

"And they were. We got them back.

"So she did have a sixth sense as to where people had gone, and where people kept things."

RALEIGH, April 20, 1943

TELEGRAM TO HONORABLE FRANKLIN D. ROOSEVELT
CARE OF PRESIDENT CAMACHO
MONTERREY, MEXICO

When your close friend, who possesses the sixth sense, read
that the Mexican Congress had given President Camacho permission to leave the country, she said: "That means he and
Franklin will hold a meeting near the border." You cannot go
beyond her knowledge of your movements. She joins in love
and we beg you to extend to President Camacho our affectionate greetings.

JOSEPHUS DANIELS

[The United States and Mexican Presidents met in secret in
Monterrey, Mexico, and Corpus Christi, Texas, in April, 1943,
to discuss war problems. Roosevelt pledged again a continuation of the Good Neighbor policy.]

RALEIGH, July 7, 1943

DEAR FRANKLIN:

I have been so disturbed over the renewed determination of
the Standard Oil Company to obtain oil in the Naval petroleum
reserves in California that I would have come to Washington
to talk with you about it if my wife had not been suffering
with renewed heart attacks. . . .

You are familiar with the attempts of the oil men to get our
Naval reserves and how strenuously we had to fight to prevent
it in the Wilson Administration, particularly their attempt in
the World War when the California Chamber of Commerce
declared that unless this reserve was made available, the State
of California would be stalled in its war effort. We defeated

all their attempts and then came the Teapot Dome and Elk Hill crime and scandal.

If the Standard should get that reserve now, I fear it will give the opposition an issue in 1944, reminiscent of the Teapot Dome. I am sure you will not permit this.

Affectionately,

JOSEPHUS DANIELS

DEAR CHIEF: WASHINGTON, July 10, 1943

I think you are absolutely right. The whole thing is stopped in California and I am quite certain there was no crookedness on the part of the Navy. The problem still remains of keeping the Standard Oil from pumping out the reserves on their section of the land.

Affectionately,

F.D.R.

DEAR FRANKLIN: RALEIGH, August 9, 1943

I was very much gratified to receive your letter giving the assurance that "the whole thing is stopped in California." I knew that would be your reaction when the matter came to your attention. I have been informed that instead of the whole thing being stopped, that 1,001,519 barrels of oil have been taken from the Naval Oil Reserve under the operations which have continued since the announcement was made that the contract had been annulled.

Of course, I have the same opinion that you have, that there was no skulduggery or corruption, but if the reserves are depleted, it will take the oil from the Navy just exactly as Fall and Doheny undertook to do. A great man once said: "The way to resume is to resume." The way to reserve the Naval oil in the ground is to reserve it.

Affectionately,

JOSEPHUS DANIELS

[Daniels was always keenly interested in oil conservation and suspicious of the big oil companies. During the war, Secretary of the Navy Frank Knox authorized the Standard Oil Company of California to drill in the Elk Hill Naval Reserve. Considerable agitation developed over the contract and the Navy cancelled it.]

WASHINGTON, December 20, 1943

TELEGRAM TO DANIELS

DEAR CHIEF: It is with a sad heart that I send you this assurance of my own sorrow in the sorrow which has been laid so heavily on you. Thank God that you had, for more than fifty years, the love and devotion and companionship of one of the noblest of women, as wife, mother, and friend. She fulfilled every duty that fell to her and leaves a memory which will be part of the imperishable heritage of all who knew her. Eleanor joins me in love and sympathy to you and all the children.

FRANKLIN D. ROOSEVELT

[Mrs. Josephus Daniels died at her home in Raleigh on December 19, 1943. A few months before her death they had celebrated their fifty-fifth wedding anniversary.]

WASHINGTON, December 13, 1944

DEAR CHIEF:

You guessed wrong in thinking that neither Eleanor nor I could snatch time to read that personally inscribed copy of your latest book: *The Wilson Era—Peace 1911–17*. Already I have read part of it and I really am going to read it through because I think it is delightful.

A prime essential of literary criticism is that the critic be wholly detached—wholly objective in his point of view. I can therefore confirm the judgment that modesty inhibited you from rendering, and declare *The Wilson Era* the best book of the year.

Seriously, there is need for just the volume which you have written and it is a happy circumstance that the author, besides having the gift of forcible and trenchant prose, had also an important part in making the history which he now has recorded in permanent form. Hearty congratulations on a job well done.

Eleanor and I will always cherish our copy. We both send you, with our heartfelt thanks, best wishes for a Holy and Happy Christmas and a New Year full of all good things.

Ever affectionately,

FRANKLIN D. ROOSEVELT

RALEIGH, March 26, 1945

DEAR FRANKLIN:

It disturbs me to see McNutt advocating further delay after the war in giving the Filipinos their long-promised independence. Wilson promised it, but Garrison and Redfield and others circumvented him and practiced mañana. And now McNutt suggests a repetition and Walter Lippmann is worse. . . .

Faithfully,

JOSEPHUS DANIELS

[Paul V. McNutt, who was to be appointed High Commissioner to the Philippines after Roosevelt's death, urged a delay in granting Philippine independence.]

WASHINGTON, April 3, 1945

DEAR CHIEF:

I do not think there is much use in delaying the independence of the Philippines and McNutt has said nothing to me about it. I would much like to have it go into effect on August thirteenth—their Fourth of July—and to go to it myself, but I fear I cannot get away for the latter because it looks now as if there will be some kind of a European conference.

I do wish you could have been in my office the other day when Jonathan was sworn in. He is a grand person and so is his wife. He is making a real hit with the Press.

I hope to see you soon.

Affectionately,

FRANKLIN D. ROOSEVELT

[Jonathan Daniels was appointed Press secretary to the President on March 24, 1945. At Roosevelt's last press conference, on April 5, 1945, F.D.R. announced: "We are absolutely unchanged in our policy of two years ago for immediate Filipino independence."]

RALEIGH, April 12, 1945

TELEGRAM TO MRS. ROOSEVELT

My heavy heart is with you in love and sympathy. You know of my love for your noble husband and our long friendship. God bless you and comfort you. Love to all the family. I will be with you in Washington on Saturday. Affectionately.

JOSEPHUS DANIELS

INDEX